T H E
FINAL CRY

Every Minute One Teenager Attempts Suicide
Every Hour One Succeeds!

THE
FINAL CRY

Greg Laurie
with Al Janssen

HARVEST HOUSE PUBLISHERS
Eugene, Oregon 97402

The names of certain persons and places mentioned in this book have been changed in order to protect the privacy of the individuals involved.

THE FINAL CRY

Copyright © 1987 by Harvest House Publishers
Eugene, Oregon 97402

Library of Congress Catalog Card Number 87-080285
ISBN 0-89081-599-2

Printed in the United States of America.

*Special thanks to Carol and John
for their hard work and faithfulness
in helping to get this book out.*

Contents

Preface

1. The Final Cry 13
2. When Will the Pain Stop? 21
3. Sex, Drugs, and Heavy Metal. 31
4. Private Battles 45
5. Taming the Wild. 57
6. All We Like Sheep. 71
7. Dealing with Peer Pressure 81
8. Handling Temptation 93
9. God's Call to the Young. 111
10. Family in Crisis 127
11. Help for Parents 137

Notes

Preface

Every so often a string of teenage suicides shocks the nation. Early one morning in March of 1987 in Bergenfield, New Jersey, two sisters and two boyfriends locked themselves in a car in the garage of an apartment complex, rolled down the windows, and breathed in the fumes from their still-running car. They took turns writing notes on a brown paper bag. Within an hour all four were dead of carbon-monoxide poisoning. The deaths were the capstone for a year in which Bergenfield had already suffered four other apparent teen suicides. One day later two girls in Illinois, apparently influenced by what had transpired in New Jersey, also took their lives by carbon-monoxide poisoning.

These stories made the headlines of our newspapers and were sensational spots on the nightly news for several days. But in time, as it always does, the story faded from public attention.

Unfortunately, the problem of teenage suicide won't go away. For teenagers today, suicide has become something of a terminal disease. And terminal will be the outcome in many more lives unless people respond to the early symptoms and warning signals. That final outcome can be avoided. But first we must recognize that teenagers are facing unprecedented difficulties and pressures. Their struggles with temptation, amplified by peer pressure to get involved in things like drugs, drinking, and sex, is extremely intense.

Contained in this book are the edited versions of a series of messages I delivered over four consecutive Sunday evenings at Harvest Christian Fellowship, the church where I pastor. Approximately 2500 people attend these meetings, and over half of them are young people. I am not an expert on the problems of teenagers, or of this tragic epidemic of teenage suicide. But I do believe that there are answers from God's

Word. The response to these messages and a subsequent video we taped for television (available for showing) has convinced me that many people desperately need to hear this message.

I anticipate that there will be two audiences reading this book. One group consists of parents who are concerned about their teenage children. The last two chapters are especially directed toward you. However, most of this book is addressed primarily to young people who must face the temptations in today's culture. I encourage parents to read *all* of it carefully. The testimonies and the message may help you better understand the struggles and obstacles that teenagers are facing today, and hopefully you will be better equipped to give them answers from God's Word. If you are the parent of a seemingly healthy teen, don't think these problems couldn't happen to you. They could! Perhaps you can learn from the mistakes of others and recognize the warning signs.

If you are a young person reading this book, I believe these messages are especially for you. If you have attempted suicide or thought about it, I want you to know there is hope. Someone cares about you. There is a reason for living, and I want to show it to you. If you have never been suicidal, don't think this book has nothing to say to you. The problems we address are ones you most likely face as well. For you, this book can be preventive medicine.

Writing this book has not been an enjoyable experience, but I believe that teenage suicide is a problem which must be faced. If this book can help save a life, or help a mother or father understand a teen or preteen, or, most importantly, help just one person enter into a relationship with the living God, then it will have been worth writing!

I have included a number of stories taken from interviews of teenagers. Many of the names and details have been changed in order to protect the privacy of those who have attempted suicide and their families.

The Final Cry

1

The Final Cry

December 7, 1941, is a day that the world remembers because of the Japanese attack on Pearl Harbor. December 7, 1985, is a day that will last a lifetime in the memories of Mark and Linda. Their experience with their 14-year-old son, Steve, typifies a tragic epidemic that is sweeping our country today.

After several separations and attempts at reconciliation, Mark and Linda were divorced when Steve was a young boy. Steve lived with his mother in San Diego but maintained a close relationship with his father, who faithfully saw him on most weekends. They would also get together on special occasions, and each summer they spent several weeks together vacationing.

Steve had a healthy interest in sports. He was physically large for his age and did well in competition. His mother was a fervent rooter for her Little League star and football star, and as Steve got older his father was also present at all his games.

Steve also showed an interest and faith in Jesus Christ, and he became involved with a church youth group. He played the part of Joseph in a church play. Acting came easy to him because it fit well with his outgoing personality, and he openly dreamed of one day becoming a disk jockey. After attending church with Steve for awhile, Mom also became a born-again Christian. Though they still faced the normal day-to-day trials, they had a common hope in the risen Savior. When Steve was 12, both of them were baptized.

Shortly after their baptism, Linda remarried. Steve "gave her away" at the wedding ceremony. They moved north to Glendora, a suburb of Los Angeles, and near where Steve's "real" father lived. For seven months Steve adjusted to his new family. Everything seemed to be progressing until he had a few run-ins at school. At that time it was decided that Steve should live with his father, where he could attend a different high school with an environment where he felt more comfortable. Both Linda and Mark felt that this would be a positive change. Steve would still visit his mother on weekends.

Once again Steve began the role of adapting to a new family. Mark had also remarried, and his wife, Judy, had a young child of her own. Steve seemed to handle most of the changes as well as could be expected by any young adolescent. His father even helped him set up some home DJ equipment so Steve could practice at home the craft he yearned to perfect one day.

It is here that the normal turns into shocking, and the memories into tears. Steve spent the first weekend in December with Linda. She went to church that Sunday morning, but Steve decided to stay home with his cousin Tim and spent the day watching videos. He was bright and cheerful when she returned home, and perhaps even more helpful than usual. He seemed unusually eager to please his mother, and she found him staring at her for long periods of time.

Thinking back now, she also recalls how Steve had grown suddenly cold and withdrawn at a wedding reception they had attended a few weeks earlier. By surprise, Steve had met up with a girl he liked. She was his "first love," and this seemed to brighten his evening at first. But after awhile he asked Linda for the keys to the car. There, in the darkness, he spent the remainder of the evening. Linda attributed Steve's behavior to the typical girlfriend playing a "hard-to-get" routine.

But Steve had already confirmed his intentions, and had in fact told friends that he wanted to die. But no one took him seriously. People simply shrugged and filed the statement away as another careless teenage comment. Steve never told his mother or father. He left his mother that early December weekend without dropping any verbal hint of his death wish.

The following Friday Steve's dad went into the hospital for a series of tests. While there he received a call from his new wife telling him that Steve had been tardy to class several times that week. Tardiness was an ongoing problem about which Mark had asked the school to keep him informed. Over the past several months Steve had also run afoul of the house rules against taking the car for a drive whenever he wanted to. Mark had dealt with Steve in a straightforward manner and had encountered the not-unexpected teenage rebellion. Though Mark was sedated due to the medical tests he was undergoing, he nonetheless had Steve come to the phone. With a typical outburst of parental anger and disgust, he let Steve know of his disappointment. Then he ordered Steve to his room, where he was to complete his homework.

It is such a "normal" combination that causes many a parent/teen relationship to develop friction. But Mark intended to call back in an hour or so, once he had calmed down, and after his abrasiveness had the desired effect on Steve. Then he would mix some love with the admonition and encouragement. It was an often-used tactic, one that seemingly worked well. But it wouldn't work this time.

Steve completed his homework assignments, then wrote two notes—one to Linda and the other to Mark. To his mother he wrote:

To Mom:

I'm sorry for all the pain I'm putting you and my dad through. I have a lot of pain too, 'cause I love you guys a lot. I might not show it, but I do. Do you think it is easy to kill yourself? Well, it's not.

It's not your fault or my dad's; it's mine 'cause I'm not good enough for you guys. Well, I'll always love you. Goodbye.

P.S. I know I won't go to heaven for killing myself. But that's what I've got to do.

Love, your son,
Steve

After his signature, he drew two teardrops. To his father he wrote:

Sorry, Dad, but I tried and still I'm not good enough for you. I know you tried, but moving me here was not right because I messed up the family. I still love you. I know you won't approve, but too late. Give my love to everybody.

Love, your son,
Steve

Steve's stepmother, Judy, left the house for ten minutes to pick up her daughter. That's when Steve loaded his father's .38 caliber pistol. When Judy returned, she noticed that the curtains in the living room had been closed. As she removed her young child from the car she heard the shot and the fall. At first she thought it had come from the neighbor's house. When she entered her home, she saw the gun case and several bullets on the couch. She raced to Steve's room. She found him on the floor, still breathing. He lived for 24 more hours.

On December 7, 1985, Steve's life came to a close. Two years later Linda still cried almost every day. No well-meaning words can ever adequately absolve her of the guilt she feels. Though she knows intellectually of God's mercy and forgiveness, her heart serves up a daily portion of unkind memories. The words she might have said, the moves, the divorce, the harsh words, the deepest of deep desires to let her son know how much he meant to her—these cross her mind every day. There are the memories of her son, from the changing of his diapers and the late-night bottle feedings to walks in the park and shopping forays to the grocery store; from skinned knees and pouting fits to hugs and bedtime prayers. All of these ended without saying goodbye. And for *no good reason*. For Linda there is not just sadness but anger, guilt, despair, and fear. There is also fear for her two younger children—fear of disciplining, fear of saying the wrong thing, fear of allowing them to face the world.

Perhaps Mark is an even greater victim. Due to the medication he was given that fateful day, the doctors would not allow him to be told the news. In the meantime Mark tried several times that night from his hospital bed to call his son back. He needed to give out those words of encouragement as badly as Steve needed to hear them. But there was no answer, and Mark was only left to guess and wonder why nobody was home. He had an awful feeling that something had gone wrong.

He was finally told late that night. After Steve died the following day, Mark cursed God for allowing such a tragedy to occur. But when he went to the police station to pick up the suicide note the following Monday, and when he found Steve's homework attached and completed, Mark cursed himself. Linda and some men from a nearby church from whom she had sought help found him clutching the blanket of Steve's bed, crying hysterically, "I killed him! I killed him!" It was only after many days of deep despair that Mark was finally able to find comfort by dedicating his life to Jesus Christ and to a service in his community that helps prevent other kids from seeking a solution through suicide.

Steve is just one example of the epidemic of teenage suicide. Every year 6000 teenagers kill themselves, and more than 600,000 try. These are not just statistics! These are people just like you and I who have been pushed to the edge. These are young people who have grown so despondent and hopeless that they believe the only way out is death.

It's high time that we expose the problems leading up to this epidemic and give some clear-cut answers that will make a difference. I write about this subject out of my own experience and background, knowing that I easily could have been a suicide victim, and knowing I was spared only by God's unfailing grace. I address this subject also because I have come to know with certainty, through experience and through the Scriptures, that suicide is more than a cop-out. It is more than an illness. It is more than a social phenomenon. I believe it is a tactic foisted upon mankind by the darkest side of the spiritual world. It is a hand grenade that has been tossed our way out of the pit of hell.

Nevertheless, there is hope. As in every form of battle, there is a strategy to employ. I have shared Steve's tragic story not just to illustrate the problem but to show that there is hope. We can learn from the backdrop of his life that there is an answer to teenage suicide. It's an answer that does not deal only with a selected aspect of an individual's life, but one that gives meaning and purpose to the question that all people face: "Why am I here?"

Others have written about this subject from a sociological perspective. Their observations are important. But the ultimate solution lies not in the physical dimension but the spiritual. Let's examine the problem and see why we need to look to God for answers.

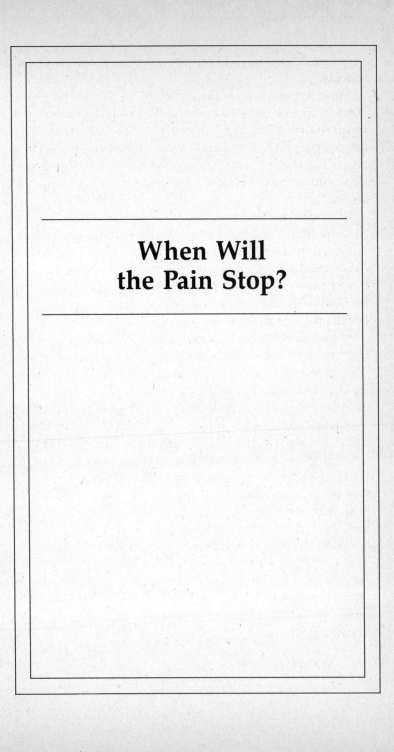

When Will
the Pain Stop?

2

When Will the Pain Stop?

Not long ago a teenager in New England walked into his high school classroom and announced to his fellow students, "You won't be seeing me anymore." Then he pulled a gun from his desk and shot himself to death. In a similar incident near my hometown, a 16-year-old boy came into his typing class one morning, sat down, pulled out a gun, and shot himself in the head.

Within the homes of Christians and non-Christians alike, young people across the country have opted out of life. Teenage suicide has tripled in the last 30 years. Actually, suicide rates may be much higher than the recognized figure of 6000 per year. Mitch Anthony, executive director of the National Suicide Help Center in Rochester, Minnesota, claims, "I would estimate it at more like 20,000. This is because many accidents—currently the leading cause of death among teenagers—are really suicides that are reported as accidents. I know of a woman whose son hung himself. Even as he hung by the rope, the police officer asked her if she wanted him to report it as an accident. I have interviewed funeral directors who have confirmed that many so-called accidents were really suicides."[1]

It's amazing how many young people are even thinking about ending their lives. In one survey, 34 percent of teenagers said they had "seriously considered" suicide, 32 percent said they had made plans, and 14 percent said they had made an attempt.[2] Another study found that 20 percent of teens said they were "empty, confused, and would rather die than live." When a group of high school and college students were asked, "Do you think suicide is ever an option for young people?" 49 percent answered "yes."[3]

When faced with these startling statistics, it's natural to think that these people are from lower-income homes and are the down-and-out of society. After all, if they had all that life has to offer, they wouldn't be despondent. But the surprising truth is that teenage suicide occurs more frequently in *middle- to upper-class* homes. One primary reason is because of the breakdown in the family structure. The following is part of a letter I received from a 16-year-old girl in response to a television program we produced on teenage suicide. She is typical of so many young people today who come from broken homes:

> I am 16. I have everything a person could want but love, understanding, and true friends. I saw your show on teenage suicide. It really got to me. I am going to turn to God. He's my last hope. I think your show really helped me. I'm just so confused. I have to try something, I just have so many problems. My arms are full of cuts, old and new. I don't have any friends. The ones I do have now are in a state hospital. I cannot talk to my family. I wish I just had anyone who really cared about me and understood how I feel, but everyone thinks I am crazy. I turned to suicide at the age of ten. At 14 I got pregnant. I wanted a baby so bad just so I could have someone to love and someone to give love back. I had twin girls, and I love them to death, but I am still depressed and have feelings of suicide and a lot of guilt. I feel like a sick tramp. Your show helped me to see how much God loves me and wants me to live.

This girl goes on to tell how one night she and three of her friends slit their wrists, and, while impatiently waiting for death to come, decided to quicken their suicide attempt by jumping onto the freeway from an overpass bridge. But before they reached their destination they were spotted by some policemen who had noticed a trail of blood. Near the end of her letter she wrote, "All I want is for the pain to stop. I want to fit in with people. I want to be happy so I can be a really good mommy. God is my last hope. If He can't help me, all I can see for my future is death." Her words could easily belong to thousands of others when she concludes, "I can't talk to my family. I have everything a person could want but love, understanding, and true friends."

Another response from a 13-year-old girl is equally disheartening. She refers to three young men we interviewed on our television special because of their experiences with suicide attempts:

> I just finished watching your show and found I could relate to many things that you said, and the other three guys that spoke. I am not a Christian. My mother believes in Buddhism, my father doesn't care for religion, and I have been raised not following any belief. Toward the end of the show my mother came downstairs and yelled at me, "TURN DOWN THE TV! IT'S STUPID NON- SENSE—THOSE PEOPLE ARE FAILURES IN LIFE!" I wanted to yell back, "Well, then, what am I?" But I was afraid that other things would leave my mouth. She didn't watch the show, but I'm sure she heard it, especially the part about how parents should show love to their children. During the past few weeks she has been telling me to go out and find another mother if she's not good enough. I say back to her, "Just wait till

I'm 16. If you don't want me, just dump me in the
trash." She says one of these days she will. That's a
conversation we have at least once a day now. . . .
I don't remember the last time I got a hug or kiss
from either parent, and I daydream about having
a boyfriend or something. I dream about people
who are really happy and huggy—you know, just
being affectionate. Please reply and I promise to
you and the Lord that I'll live until then.

Why are so many of today's teenagers feeling this way?
Perhaps the most significant reason for this epidemic is the
lack of roots in the home. The family structure has continued to crumble in recent years. Many teenagers are being
cared for by parents who were products of the "me" generation of the sixties. In their personal pursuit of wealth and
pleasure these parents often treat their kids as nothing
more than excess baggage. Ann Landers once asked this
question of parents: If you knew then what you know now,
would you still have children? Of those who responded,
70 percent said "no"!

In addition, because of the post-World-War-II baby boom,
there are simply more people in America than ever before.
That means more competition—for grades, colleges, jobs,
and attention. During this time of increased pressure,
teenagers are getting less support. Roughly half of all first
marriages end in divorce, which means that many children
today grow up in single-parent households, or with one
natural parent and a stepparent. Families are moving more
often, and with the increase of two-career families parents
are spending less time with their children. One Boston
survey found that fathers spend an average of 37 *seconds* a
day with an infant![4]

Is it any wonder that our kids feel so despondent? Is it
any wonder that they sense they are unloved? Is it any
wonder that they turn to their peers for direction, and as a

result engage in drugs, alcohol, and sexual permissiveness? And is it any wonder that when these influences don't fill the emptiness in their lives, they consider suicide?

Some people are even asking the question, "Is suicide contagious?" Recent events might lead us to answer an unfortunate "yes." A pattern of "cluster" suicides has sprung up across our nation. During a 12-month period starting in February 1983, seven teenagers in Plano, Texas, committed suicide—four by carbon-monoxide poisoning and three by guns. Five boys in Westchester and Putnam Counties of New York died by their own hands in February 1984, four of them by hanging. *Time* magazine ran an article in February 1986 about a school in Omaha, Nebraska, that was branded "Suicide High" when three students killed themselves and four others tried to do so.

Then there were the highly publicized "copycat" suicides that rocked the nation in March of 1987. It began in Bergenfield, New Jersey, when two sisters (ages 17 and 18) and two boys (18 and 19) locked themselves in a car in the garage of an apartment complex and died of carbon-monoxide poisoning. One day later two girls in Illinois, apparently influenced by what had transpired in New Jersey, also took their lives by carbon-monoxide poisoning.

Nationally, the media has spared no effort to cover this epidemic. Magazines such as *Time, Newsweek, Rolling Stone,* and *Seventeen* have probed and poked for answers. At least one made-for-TV movie has worked with this sensational theme. But while many people have joined the chorus to ask "why?" few have offered answers for the American teenager.

Among the fragmented bits of knowledge and wisdom offered by psychologists, psychiatrists, medical doctors, law-enforcement agencies, social groups, and media talk-show hosts have come few definitive answers. The experts are groping. For teens in our society, choosing to pull the trigger, to tighten the noose, to slash the wrists, or to run the garden hose from the tailpipe to the car window has become the ultimate final statement. Pulling the plug ends all the arguments. Is there anything that can motivate these kids to live?

My answer is a resounding "yes!" No matter how hopeless the situation, there is an alternative to suicide. Sadly, I don't think any real answers are being given to children from the so-called experts or in our public schools. The reason kids aren't finding the answers is because the most important ingredient is lacking. The American dream is looking like a sham. The dream of life, liberty, and the pursuit of happiness has become empty and void. When all the statistics and all the medical and psychological analyses are in, the common dimension that all suicidal persons face ultimately rests in dealing with the void that every person experiences. That void can only be filled by God.

Of course some people will be quick to say that this is an unrealistic "quick fix." Many social, medical, and psychological experts concede that if "religion" works for an individual, then fine; but they quickly add that it's not for everyone. Others go even farther and point out that the kind of depression that leads to suicide is often biologically induced, and therefore spiritual remedies are simply not applicable. But I must respond with this question: Does this minimize God's importance in the life of a suicidal person? Does it diminish the responsibility on the part of every individual to accept the biblical position that every man, woman, teenager, and child is separated from God by a sinful nature and can only find permanent help for his condition in the person of Jesus Christ? Every teenager and adult, whether suicidal or not, needs to know God in a real and personal way.

In 1984 Harvest Ministries produced a half-hour video on teenage suicide that was shown on television in several cities. In that special program were three testimonies by teenagers who had attempted suicide but then found that

Jesus Christ could fill the void in their lives. I clearly presented the alternative, the hope that is only found in Jesus Christ. The letters and phone calls we've received from that television special have confirmed that this message can literally save lives. On one night alone there were 13 suicides prevented by that program—that's what we were told by people who called the number on our screen.

One 19-year-old who called was a member of a hard-rock band. He was cleaning his gun in preparation to kill himself while his brother watched our program. His brother urged him to call the number, which he did. After talking to the counselor, the young man gave his heart to the Lord and put the gun away for good.

A 16-year-old boy who had just been released from juvenile hall was considering taking his life. He said he had attempted suicide 22 times. He was first put in juvenile hall when he was ten years old for trying to kill his mother with a pellet gun. He said his mother was an alcoholic and had physically abused him. He prayed with the counselor and accepted Jesus Christ, then agreed to begin counseling the next day.

A 19-year-old called while in the process of taking his life with sleeping pills. He was involved in a homosexual relationship and was taking drugs and alcohol to hide the pain. While the counselor was on the phone, the young man prayed, then flushed the pills down the toilet and said he would call back the next day. He did so, and agreed to consider further counseling.

Not all the calls have such satisfying conclusions. A 13-year-old girl from Los Angeles called and was going to take her life that night because her father had been sexually molesting her. But she hung up on us because her father was asleep and she was afraid he would wake up and start it all over again.

A teenage girl wrote to us to say, "You have made me realize that there is so much in life, even if one of them steers me into suicide. You have reached me in time to tell me that life must go on. I don't think about suicide anymore. The booklet that I received from 'A New Beginning' (the name of our television program) has really changed my life. I have never really thought about church but I would like to go."

Such responses demonstrate that there is a spiritual answer to this problem. But how does this message penetrate the hearts and minds of a society so callous to the ways of God? Perhaps we need to try to understand the social climate in which today's teenagers live.

Sex, Drugs,
and Heavy Metal

3

Sex, Drugs, and Heavy Metal

Why are so many teenagers determined to take their own lives? While this is a complicated issue with no pat answers, some common threads are apparent when we talk with young people who have attempted suicide. In this chapter I want to examine three major elements of the social climate among teens today—sex, drugs, and rock 'n' roll. In the next chapter I will look at the more private forces of family, loneliness, and hopelessness.

Why are young people involved in the big three? Why are they getting sexually involved with each other? Why are they taking drugs? Why do they listen to heavy-metal bands? Studies show that the primary reason is *peer pressure*. "It's the thing—everybody is doing it," they say. A second reason is to escape from the pressures of life. Third, but further back, they do it "for kicks" or "to have a good time." Let's look at these three major areas and listen to some teenagers who are well acquainted with these activities.

Teenage Sex

Recently I read the following statement: "The typical high school student today encounters more sexual temptation on his way to and from school than his grandfather ever found when he was out as a young boy on Saturday night looking for it."[1] The teenage sex problem is so bad right now that 80 percent of all teenage boys and 70 percent

31

of all teenage girls have sex before graduation from high school.[2] As a result 1.1 million teenage girls become pregnant each year. If the present trend continues, 40 percent of today's 14-year-old girls will be pregnant at least once before the age of 20![3]

One 15-year-old girl, when asked why she had sex, said, "I wasn't able to handle the pressure. I was part of a group of people in junior high that were into partying and hanging out." She went on to say that she started having sex with her boyfriend, but "it was a real downer because it was against what I really was." In other words, she didn't really want to do it. Yet it was important for her to be part of the group, and since everyone was having sex, she felt she had to also. Pressure is felt through comments like "Hey, have you . . . you know . . . done IT yet?" And if you haven't, then "What? What's wrong with you?"

To compound this problem, we're learning that most sexual activity is not happening in the backseat of the car like it did in the "old days." Now it happens between the hours of two and six in the afternoon—after school and while Mom and Dad are at work. The combination of "latchkey kids" and the acceptance of premarital sex in our society provides a strong temptation for today's teens. Premarital and extramarital sex are routinely portrayed in the story lines of nearly all soap operas and many network prime time TV shows. Nobody wants to say it's wrong! Consequently, we see the results of a society that condones uncontrolled passion.

Many girls engage in sex not because they want it but because it is one way to get the affection they don't have at home. I think this was clearly demonstrated in the last chapter from this letter I received in response to our program. You'll remember that the girl wrote, "I don't remember the last time I got a hug or kiss from either parent, and I daydream about having a boyfriend or something, I dream about people who are really happy and huggy—you know, just being affectionate." She asked for help and closed with this haunting line: "I promise to you and the Lord that I'll live until then."

This craving for affection reminds me of a story about another woman I met. Rhonda was the last of 12 children. Her parents were pastors in a radical Christian group. Though she knew her mother loved her, Rhonda was also very aware that she wasn't wanted. She was pretty much allowed to fend for herself.

When Rhonda was 11, her mother died. That's when life became a nightmare for this girl. She was mad at God for taking away her mother, and even madder when her father ran off with one of the ladies in the church. She looked around and saw that many church members were unfaithful to their spouses. "I got into the thing of wanting love so badly that I gave myself to anybody and everybody, even old men," she told us. "I didn't think it was wrong because my father even did this type of thing. I didn't understand, and I thought, 'Well, I guess this is what you do.' Yet in my heart I felt conviction."

It didn't take long before she was thoroughly depressed about life. After being shunted around among her older brothers and sisters, she wound up as a young teenager living alone in a trailer behind the home of one of her older sisters. "I knew the Lord and I prayed earnestly. I begged Him saying, 'God, don't wake me up tomorrow. Just take me home. I have no reason to live.' But God didn't do that. He allowed me to go through even more tragedies of rape and molestation. I just couldn't understand why. So I started toying with the idea of death.

"Finally one morning I said, 'God, forgive me, but if You won't take me, I have to do it myself.' I remember going to the medicine cabinet and pulling out all of these pills. I just took them all and I slept for days. I thought maybe if I went to sleep peacefully I would wake up in the Lord's arms. Then I remember my nephew pounding on the door and I jumped up and it seemed really strange. He said, 'Where have you been?' and I said, 'I don't know.' The Lord didn't let me die."

Rhonda tried again a few weeks later, but again she lived. So she gave up and began going to bars and dancing for money. But over the years she got sick of one-night stands and longed to find her true love.

We must admit that sex has simply gotten out of control. The spread of herpes and AIDS is cause for great alarm. Yet people are still not addressing the real problem by defining it according to the absolutes that God has laid out in His original plan. Sex, any sex, outside of God's institution of marriage is WRONG! *What we need today is not so much birth control but self-control.*

Drugs

Another enormous problem today is drugs. In more than 50 percent of suicides or suicide attempts, drugs are either part of the person's history or part of the actual attempt. A recent report in *USA Today* noted that teens who commit suicide today are ten times more likely to be drunk or high on drugs than were their counterparts of 20 years ago.

Keith, a 19-year-old youth in our church, says he was brought to the point of attempting suicide because of drug abuse. "I was doing Christmas Trees, which is a form of speed. I was addicted to them, and you have to keep taking more and more and more to get to the same high that you want. I was afraid of taking any downers because I was afraid my heart would stop and I would die. Yet I was doing so much speed that I wanted to kill myself. It got to the point where I couldn't handle it anymore. You have to keep pressing forward and you gotta keep doing things and yet your body is deteriorating inside from no sleep and from so much activity that your heart can't handle the pressure anymore, and it feels like it is just going to explode."

He wound up on a couch, trying to cut his wrists with a

butcher knife. It seemed like the only way out to him. Why? Because he felt that nobody cared. He looked at his life, his family, his friends, and saw nothing but failure. All his fantasies of becoming someone special, "Mr. Famous," were shattered. At this point God literally intervened. Somewhere, at some time, someone had told Keith about God's love. As the knife was starting to dig into his wrists, this thought came to him: "Jesus has already given His life. I don't have to take mine."

Mark is another 19-year-old who attempted suicide with a combination of drugs, alcohol, and slashing his wrists. He was six years old when his parents were divorced. Initially that didn't affect him, but as he grew older he missed the love of his parents. "We all need structure in life," he says, "and when we don't know how to go about it, we need somebody to tell us." At least one reason he started taking drugs was to cover his guilt. "I felt really guilty about the things I was doing. I was rebelling, and I was hurting my father and really hurting my mom, who was trying very hard to help me. The guilt triggered me to do more damage. I continued with violence, drugs, and really heavy into rock 'n' roll and parties. The drugs helped me hide from the world. I would just get inside myself and drift away. The music also helped; the rock bands really understood the way I felt."

Listen as Mark describes why he attempted suicide: "I wanted to escape. I wanted to get away from the pain, from all the damage I had done to other people, and the only way seemed to be this little dark hole that I could envision in my mind. Looking at that hole, I just told myself that this was it, and that's why I tried to kill myself. I was trying to get away from all the ugliness that I saw in my life. I tried and almost succeeded. It was very close, but it seemed the Lord didn't want me to die."

One California poll found that 27 percent of all teenagers admit smoking marijuana, and that figure zooms to

39 percent among those over 15. Another study, by the American Academy of Pediatrics, says that medical experts have determined that the levels in marijuana have increased as much as 25 times over what they were in the 1960's.

Meanwhile, some 28 percent of teenagers nationwide have tried cocaine—and that includes 60,000 12- and 13-year-olds. There is a new form of cocaine now on the streets called "crack," and it's used excessively by kids. It is one of the most addictive drugs known to man. So we see that sex is out of control and drugs are out of control. A third factor is a powerful force in the first two activities. Mark alluded to it when he talked about his use of drugs. It's the area of music.

Rock 'n' Roll

One of the most dramatic scenes in our video about teenage suicide is a statement by John Tanner. This young man has had numerous operations in an attempt to repair his face, which he tried to blow off with a shotgun. Listen to his haunting words:

> I wasn't thinking realistically. One of my favorite songs at that time was "Killing Yourself" by Black Sabbath. That day I skipped school and listened to rock music all day long. About a quarter after five I took the shotgun, which I'd loaded two days before, put the barrels to my chin, and pulled the trigger. The blast blew off my jaw, nose, tongue, and roof of my mouth. It wasn't what I thought it would be. I've wasted ten years of my life and have nothing to show for it but a messed-up face.

Before heading into this controversial subject, I should say that I'm not a preacher standing on a soapbox saying that anything with a beat is of the devil and shouldn't be listened to. What I *do* want to say can be summed up this way: We are foolish if we naively think that music is just music, and that it's all innocent. We've got to pay attention to what's being put out there for kids to listen to today. It's not *all* bad, and it's not *all* horrible. But a lot of the lyrical content in rock 'n' roll songs—specifically those from the heavy-metal bands—are blatantly pushing a satanic message.

Keith told us that he got involved with drugs mainly through rock concerts. When he was younger, he wasn't that interested in rock music. "I was into more mellow stuff," he says. "You slowly get pulled into heavier rock 'n' roll. I started going to concerts and getting backstage passes and talking to these people. I still wasn't doing drugs at this point, but seeing more and more people around me that were doing them said to me, 'this is okay. You are going to get a great feeling out of it. It's going to turn your life around and you can get rid of your problems by doing drugs.' You can't, of course, but I didn't realize that. I kept going to the concerts and slowly got involved in doing speed and some pot."

He was right about drugs not solving his problems. He talks about them pulling him into "stillness, a deadness, to where all you can think about is nobody cares about you, so you want to take your life. You just want to escape this world."

The music he listened to only encouraged such thinking. He says that ultimately the heavy-metal bands were an influence on his life. Many of them sing about suicide. "They're saying it's okay to kill yourself. I don't think all heavy-metal bands are satanic, but they know that Satan sells. They do stage acts to promote Satan."

But it's not a game. While it wouldn't be fair to condemn all the individuals who make up these and other popular heavy-metal bands, there are nevertheless reasons for concern. I had an opportunity while in Japan to meet and talk with one of the members of a very popular heavy-metal band, and I found his reaction to the gospel very interesting. Our paths crossed at the Tokyo Airport. I was on a speaking tour and they were doing a series of concerts. I started talking to the lead guitarist for the group and told him about how he needed to have a personal encounter with the Lord. He told me how he was raised in the church as a child, but lost interest because of the rules and regulations. Since he and his group had achieved a great measure of success, he wasn't interested in God any longer.

While the two of us talked, the other members of the group were looking over at me and sneering. It was obvious that I wasn't winning any bonus points with them. I continued to share with the lead guitarist until he suddenly stopped the conversation. It seemed as though he wanted to prove to the others that he wasn't caving in to my Christian message. So he held up his hand, which had a ring with a symbol that I had never seen before, and he said, "This is what I'm into; leave me alone!" As I looked at him, his whole countenance changed and he started saying repeatedly, "Get out of here! Get out of here!" I felt at that moment an unmistakable presence of evil.

I believe that much of today's heavy-metal music is opening the door for kids to enter into the satanic realm. Most kids will tell you, "I'm not into Satan; I just like the music." They think it's pretty cool to wear a black T-shirt with a pentagram—a symbol of the satanic church—or "666" emblazoned across it because it's bound to get a reaction from Mom and Dad. That's why they love it. When I was a teenager, the more my friends and I could shock the adults, the better. Today the chains and spikes and black leather associated with heavy metal and rebellion makes parents cringe.

But this is more serious than simply shocking the adults. Kids don't realize that they are literally playing with fire. The Bible says, "Can a man take fire to his bosom and . . . not be burned?" (Proverbs 6:27). Those satanic symbols and the evil power which those bands are singing about are becoming more than just lyrics. Surely some of the listeners are bound to think, "Maybe they have something to say. Maybe this is something that offers an answer." They are playing with darkness, and darkness is gaining a foothold in their lives.

I believe the devil today is speaking into the ears of teenagers, telling them to end their lives. In much of the current heavy-metal music, suicide is pictured as an alluring alternative.

Something that we don't hear reported much—but it's becoming more common—is the so-called "metal-murder" phenomenon. I've talked with policemen on several forces in Southern California who verify that these types of murders are thought to be influenced by heavy-metal music. They include such atrocities as animal sacrifice, graveyard rituals, and perverse sex. One case that did come to the public eye in 1985 was the much-publicized "Night Stalker" murders. One of the clues left behind at the site of one murder were the letters "AC/DC" scrawled in blood on one of the walls. It was a reference to the heavy-metal band by the same name. A random sample of some of the group's song titles reveals what they stand for: "Highway to Hell," "Hell Ain't a Bad Place to Be," "Shoot to Thrill," "Overdose," and "If You Want Blood (You've Got It)."

I believe this is just the tip of the iceberg. If we knew fully what was going on in our country today, I think it would curl our hair. That's why even playing games like Dungeons and Dragons or watching some of the Saturday-morning cartoons that are heavily flavored toward occultism can prove dangerous. These "innocent" types of fun actually open the door for inquisitive kids to begin probing into areas that may prove harmful and even deadly.

What about those kids who fall for these heavy-metal

lyrics and try to take their lives? I wish they could be present to find out what really happens after they commit suicide. It's not as romantic or as beautiful as the lie they've been led to believe. I wish they could see the anguish when, after they've taken a shotgun and blasted it into their face, their parents are left behind to scrape up the pieces. I wish they could see the funeral service where their friends can only shake their heads and wonder. I wish they could see how soon they're forgotten by those friends who go on living. I wish they could see how that last great statement is so easily undone and forgotten.

Some of their friends might reason, "But their pain is over now. They'll go on to a better life." How can one be certain of that? There is also a very real place called hell, which the Bible describes as a place of torment. What guarantee does anyone have who has been listening to Satan that he won't end up eternally in hell? Might Satan's whispers of "I'll take good care of you" be a lie? For many who seek to end the pain through death, I fear they will discover that the pain is only beginning.

Fortunately, the youngsters we've quoted in this chapter have found the answer. It's not in suicide but in a personal relationship with Jesus Christ. Keith heard the truth of God's message—that Jesus Christ gave His life so that Keith didn't have to take his life. "God made me feel accepted," he says, "because He gave me things that I never deserved. He died for me and gave His life, and I wasn't even willing to give my own life to friends around me or to my own family. I was looking out for number one. God has turned me around. It wasn't instantaneous. All He asked for was my heart; He didn't ask for anything else. He has given me love and an answer to my life."

Rhonda admits that her problem was looking at *people* instead of God. As she saw the hypocrisy around her, she lost all desire to live. Although she never gave up her church life, she now admits, "I lived a double life. Finally the Lord sent Craig; I finally met the man I had earnestly prayed for. We both felt we were Christians, but we weren't into the Word." They are now both attending church and studying the Scriptures. For Rhonda the nightmare is over. What she never experienced in her one-night stands she has found in a relationship with Christ—true love.

Private Battles

4

Private Battles

In an article from *Newsweek* about children of broken homes, this is what one eight-year-old girl said about her parents' divorce:

> I remember it was near my birthday and I was going to be six, and Dad said at lunch he was leaving. I tried to say, "No, Dad, don't do it," but I couldn't get my voice out—I was too shocked. All the fun things we had done flashed right out of my head and all the bad things came in, like when we had to go to the hospital with his bad back and he got mad at me. The bad thoughts just stuck there. My life sort of changed at that moment, like I used to be always happy and suddenly I was sad.[1]

The article went on to name divorce as one of the most serious and complex mental health problems facing children of the 1980's. The numbers alone are formidable: Currently there are 12 million children under the age of 18 whose parents are divorced. Roughly one million children a year suffer through the dissolution of their family.

We cannot talk about teenage suicide without recognizing that the family is a major factor contributing to this epidemic. Approximately 71 percent of young people who attempt suicide are from broken homes. In one study,

75 percent of teens from broken homes reported that they felt guilty and responsible for the divorce.[2]

In spite of the saying that children are like an old saw—flexible enough to learn to cope and bounce back—evidence suggests that the impact of divorce and the resulting period of adjustment is both painful and damaging. The drama of divorce is second only to death, says child psychologist Lee Salk.[3] Children sense a deep loss and feel they are suddenly vulnerable to forces beyond their control. Research shows that children between the ages of six and eight assume responsibility for the split between their parents. It is clear that children have fears of being abandoned, and though they're old enough to realize what's going on, they don't have adequate skills to deal with it.[4]

Even when families do not split, there is frequently tension that causes children to feel isolated. A 1985 study by the American Academy of Pediatrics found that "90 percent of suicidal adolescents believed that their families did not understand them. The adolescents felt isolated and anonymous. They also believed that their efforts to communicate feelings of unhappiness, frustration, or failure were ignored or denied by parents who strive for their children to be the successes they were unable to become." Such information only underscores the need for teenagers to find some degree of common ground with their parents. Instead, many teens are finding empty homes and consequently empty hearts.

Children aren't turning to their parents any longer, often because there are no parents to turn to or else because their parents are just too busy. A survey by the University of Minnesota examined who or what kids in trouble will turn to for help. They discovered that today's teens will turn to music, drugs, friends, and even video games before they go to their parents or other adults to discuss their problems. It's a little disheartening as a parent to know that you're getting beat out by PacMan! The study showed that out of 54 coping options, mothers ranked number 31 and dads were almost at the bottom, ranking 48th![5]

Lance is a 15-year-old boy who tried to kill himself because "the stress was unbearable." His parents were divorced when he was in sixth grade, but the family problems had actually begun much earlier. He had his first experience with pot in fourth grade and started drinking in fifth grade. "I had no father figure in my life," he says. "I was just going with the flow, as they say. I just lived; I didn't live for a purpose."

The pressure he's felt as a teenager has at times bordered on resentment. A youngster shouldn't have to cope with such stress. He mentions the peer pressure, and how he smoked pot and drank just to feel a sense of belonging that he should have had from his family. Listen as Lance explains.

> After we moved to California, we used to sit down and have dinner and talk during dinner. We just stopped doing that and that's when the downpour started. That's when my brother started acting up. When we didn't discuss anything, we walked in, we ate, we slept in the house, and that's all we used it for. It's like we were boarders; we weren't a family. And that's something a kid really needs today. It's not that it's my mother's fault or that it's my father's fault, because they had their own problems. But I still think maybe they should talk more to the kids because that's what we really need is to talk, whether it's about what happened at school today or about the dance or about a boyfriend or a girlfriend or anything. And then when you have a big problem, you have somebody to talk to. It's not so hard. If you talk every night about the baseball game you had during the afternoon, it's not so hard to bring in

something else out of the blue, like drugs, or even Christ.

I think the reason I started smoking pot and drinking was to get attention—to get the affection that I never really got at home. What I wanted from my parents was affection and attention, to be talked to, loved, and hugged—stuff that I really never got at home. I missed that so much because touching is so vital to everybody.

Some of the best times I remember are when we used to spend time as a family just doing anything—going on camping trips or going to a fun park or taking a picnic or anything. We always used to do those things when I was little, and I remember almost all of them. I remember how happy I was. But then as I got older they decreased. Fishing trips are just as important to a 16-year-old kid as they are to a nine-year-old kid.

The hardest part, what made me feel like dying, was the pain—it hurt. It was just a gut feeling that was with you all the time, when you went to bed and then when you got up in the morning; it's like you couldn't shake it. I mean you would get in good moods and something nice would happen and you'd laugh, and then boom! you're right down into it again. It hurts so bad, and you don't know how to get with it. There's no drug you can take (there is, but it only covers it for a couple of hours) because then it's there again and you don't know what to do. All you want to do is die.

Lance started contemplating suicide when he was in seventh grade. It kept building. At first he thought about it once a month. Then once every two weeks. Then once a week. Finally he was thinking about it every day. Fortunately, Lance never reached the point where he actually made an attempt on his life, because he started noticing three people who were different. They were Christians, and Lance noticed how great their lives were and how he wanted what they had. He was walking home one day after school, thinking about how bad his life was and how he wanted to die. He considered throwing himself in front of a car in the street. Then he thought again of his three friends and realized that he had another choice.

> I said straight out, "Jesus Christ, You've got your chance." At that point, such a power came over me that it's unexplainable. It's such a great high feeling that it's better than any drug you could ever take or any alcohol you could ever drink. It's something in your heart and your body and your mind and your soul, everywhere. He came in! Now I have Somebody to talk to; I have a male figure in my life, Somebody to love me and to give me affection without having to take drugs or drink alcohol or do stupid things.

I think it's quite obvious that the American family is in a crisis today. Marriage, the cornerstone of family life, is coming apart at the seams. This breakdown of the family has a definite effect on the children involved. In addition, or perhaps as a result, we find many teenagers trying to cope with loneliness.

Loneliness

One psychiatrist has stated that loneliness is the most devastating malady of our age. Loneliness leaves people unfulfilled, unloved, and surrounded by doubts and fears. This chronic loneliness involves feelings of inner emptiness, sadness, discouragement, restlessness, anxiety, isolation, and an intense desire to be wanted or needed by someone. Lonely people feel unwanted, left out, and rejected even when they are surrounded by other people. Ultimately this can cause people to consider self-destruction.

Kim is a Japanese-American girl who tried to drown herself. "I came to the conclusion that nobody loved me," she says. "Then I thought about how my parents love me—at least they say they do, and my friends kinda say they do—and then I came to the conclusion that even if they could love me, they couldn't fill me up. It wouldn't fill up that emptiness that was inside of me."

An interesting aspect of Kim's story is that she thought she was a Christian. She attended church and a youth group, but she admits now that she wasn't a Christian because "my life didn't change. When I was at school I'd be a jerk to my friends and cuss and I wasn't a very nice person. But I'd go to church and I would be the holiest person in the world. I knew all the things you need to know. I could answer all the questions. They were preaching the gospel, but they just assumed that I was a Christian, so they didn't direct it toward me." It was after her attempted suicide that Kim really gave her life to Jesus Christ and found the answer to her loneliness.

To the lonely person Jesus says, "I will never leave you nor forsake you" (Hebrews 13:5). Actually, that passage could literally be translated, "I will never, no never, no NEVER leave you or forsake you." Kim and other teenagers have discovered that their parents may leave them and their closest friends may desert them, but Jesus promises, "Lo, I am with you always, even to the end of the age" (Matthew 28:20). The book of Proverbs describes Him as a Friend who sticks closer than a brother. It's great to know that we are not alone, no matter where we are; God is there with us and will give us the courage to face anything. There is a God who is relentless in His pursuit of lonely and hurting people.

Another reason for teenagers taking their lives is low self-image. Parents push their children to be high achievers, to get good grades, to make the team, to prove themselves. Sometimes they push too hard. I read recently of a 12-year-old girl from Orange County in Southern California who outwardly was everything a parent could want a daughter to be. She had a 3.3 grade-point average and talked about going to college. She was a cheerleader and was popular and attractive. But she took her life. The girl's mother said, "She was all the things you'd want your daughter to be, but that's not what it's all about. Those achievements are of little satisfaction. They're only there for a moment." Instead, she said parents should let their children know, "We love you for *who* and *what* you are, not for your achievements."

I couldn't agree with this parent more. Each teenager needs to know that he or she has tremendous potential, which in many cases lies untapped. You see, each of us is created in the image of God, but sadly that image has been gravely marred by sin. Sin is not just doing what is wrong, but literally it means "to miss the mark." The Bible teaches that we all sin (miss the mark) and fall short of God's glory. We may try to improve ourselves, believe in ourselves, and live as morally as possible, but we still miss the mark. Too often teenagers are told that they need self-esteem when what they really need is "God-esteem." A teenager who is lonely, depressed, and despondent needs his or her sin cleansed. He needs to find a relationship with Christ, who in turn will give him a sense of worth and purpose.

Unfortunately, many teenagers have just the opposite— they live with a sense of utter hopelessness.

Hopelessness

All of these factors that we've examined—sex, drugs, rock 'n' roll, family breakdown, and loneliness—lead to feelings of pure hopelessness for many of today's teens. I received the following letter from a 19-year-old girl:

I believe in Jesus but I feel that He does not

believe in me. I have tried to take the easy out but just couldn't do it. I don't know why. My insides are so empty sometimes that I don't want to wake up in the morning. I just want to sleep all day.

My family is upper-middle-class, and two of my friends killed themselves in the past year. . . . I have one question to ask: Do you think Jesus will ever answer me? I'm about ready to give up.

Yes, Jesus will answer, and we will see how in this book. But it's not surprising that teenagers wonder. As they look beyond themselves at the outside world, their personal struggles appear even more hopeless. On any given day a teenager can pick up a newspaper or turn on a television set and learn about war in the Middle East, starvation in Africa, and a smorgasbord of murders, muggings, accidents, and natural disasters. Fueled by television, violence has become an accepted condition of life in America. The average child will have seen 17,000 violent deaths on TV by the time he or she enters college!

Hovering over all of this is the threat of global suicide. Rabbi Earl Grollman, who has written several books on death and suicide, says, "Kids are actually living with a sword over their heads." Having to face so much with drugs, alcohol, illicit sex, and now threats of annihilation, is it any wonder that they feel "Why not? What else is there?" In fact the great question that many teens are asking today is not "Is there life after death?" but the question that I used to ask when I was a kid: "Is there life during life?"

What's often confusing is that the person who is contemplating suicide conveys conflicting messages. Often following a suicide the survivors are stunned because the victim was thought to be doing well. It's not unusual for a victim to seem happy and talkative right up to the day of his death. Frequently friends will say, "I saw him just this week and he was really happy. In fact he gave me his bicycle and his records." Only too late do they realize that those gestures were actually a last will and testament.

What follows is a partial list of some of the critical warning signs that are evident in a young person who senses utter hopelessness and is thinking about committing suicide:

1. Withdrawal from family or friends.
2. A change in sleeping and eating habits.
3. Persistent boredom or difficulty concentrating.
4. A decline in the quality of schoolwork.
5. Violent or rebellious behavior.
6. Radical personality changes.
7. Running away.
8. Drug and/or alcohol abuse.
9. Unusual neglect of appearance.
10. Preoccupation with themes of death.
11. Giving away prized possessions.
12. Expressing suicidal thoughts, even jokingly.

A major question that people have when faced with a potentially suicidal person is "Will confrontation push him over the edge?" Most experts agree that if we sense despondency in another person, or notice any of the critical signs mentioned above, we should confront him. In fact, when these people are confronted, they are usually diverted from suicide rather than driven to it.

What is it that we can offer these teenagers who feel such hopelessness that they are driven to consider their self-destruction? They need to see that there *is* hope. Jesus promises us that He will come again and establish His kingdom on this earth. The Bible calls this our blessed hope. Jesus Christ is our hope. Though we may not know *what* the future holds, we know *who* holds the future. If you are a young person who has come from a broken home,

Jesus can give you the love that your father or your mother was never able to give you.

The Bible describes God as "our Father who art in heaven." He can be a Father for you. He is Someone you can look up to and love and respect. He is Someone who will protect you in life. The Old Testament hero, King David, wrote, "When my father and my mother forsake me, then the Lord will take care of me" (Psalm 27:10). David knew what it was like to come from a difficult home. Early in his life, his father would not even admit that he had a young son named David. He treated him as though he weren't even alive. Doesn't that sound like the treatment so many young people receive today? Yet David said that even when his parents forsook him, God was still there. We can enter into a relationship with God that will completely fill that longing of loneliness or hopelessness.

As I've done research, trying to learn why teenagers are taking their lives, I've found that many of the traits were prevalent in my own life as a teenager. Had it not been for divine intervention, I might have wound up as another statistic.

Taming the Wild

5

Taming the Wild

By now you realize that I believe the solution to teen suicide is an encounter with the person of Jesus Christ. By this I'm not talking about "religion"; I mean a *relationship* with the living God. I have read polls that say most teenagers believe in God. The average teenager is probably a lot like Kim in the last chapter: She believed in God and therefore she assumed she was a Christian. But would she and many other teenagers be turning to alcoholism, drug abuse, sexual immorality, and ultimately suicide if they truly had a *relationship* with the living God through Jesus Christ?

I believe there are many kids who think they have already tried the route of religion. In many cases they have experienced nothing more than some rules and regulations, or perhaps some meaningless religious ritual. But I doubt whether they have really been confronted with the facts of the gospel. There is a tendency in this country to think that we've heard the gospel many times. I don't think that is necessarily true. We've heard a lot about *religion*, and we've heard a lot of *preaching*, but I question how often we've heard the true gospel—the simple truth that Jesus died on the cross for our sins, that He rose again from the dead, and that He is coming again soon.

Jesus can radically change a person's life *if* that person will submit his heart so that Jesus can cleanse him of all sin. I don't believe young people today are hearing that truth often enough. Many young people have never had these truths presented to them. There are some in the church who contend that teenagers don't want to hear such a hardline gospel, that they prefer it candy-coated and watered down. But from my own experience of speaking to teenagers for more than 15 years, I have found the opposite to be true.

When I was a kid, I used to hang around Newport Beach in Southern California and laugh at the long-haired, wild-eyed religious fanatics. Those were the days of hippies and Jesus freaks, and while I was sympathetic to the former, I was hostile to the latter. Occasionally a bold one would venture to talk to me, usually by trying to read me a gospel tract. I would reluctantly grab the booklet and stuff it in my pocket. My hostile expression would then warn him to leave me alone. But despite my hardness, I never once threw any of those booklets away. I stuffed them in a drawer at home, and periodically I would pull them out and try to figure out what this religious stuff was. I really wanted to know God, if that was indeed possible, but no one had ever explained to me how Jesus can change a person's life. Of course, I hadn't given anyone much of a chance to do any explaining.

Ironically, I thought I was a Christian because I believed in a supreme being. Whenever I was in trouble I would ask God for help. One day I was driving home from Laguna Beach above some rocky cliffs with several friends and a kilo of marijuana hidden in the trunk of our car. It was raining and the road was slippery. Suddenly I felt the car begin to fishtail. As the car went out of control I distinctly remember saying, "O God, if You're there, help, please!" I could envision headlines in the next morning's paper: "Drug Pushers Killed in Car Accident." (Actually, we weren't pushers; we planned to smoke all of that grass ourselves!) I could imagine people reading that and saying, "It serves them right." I prayed, "God, I'll do anything. I'll be a priest, a missionary, anything You want. Just get me out of this." The car stopped swerving, but as we returned to the proper lane my attitude changed immediately. "Thanks, God; see you next accident." That was the sum total of my so-called Christianity: asking God for help when I got in over my head.

If any teenager was ever a candidate for suicide, I certainly was. We have talked about drugs, rock music, broken families, loneliness, and hopelessness; all of these things were part of my life.

I came from a broken home. My mother was married and divorced a number of times. As a result I was carted around the country like a piece of excess baggage. I never knew a man I could really call my father. In addition, my mother was an alcoholic. It wasn't uncommon to find her passed out when I came home, so I would have to fix my own food. There were nights when she wouldn't even come home, and as a seven-year-old boy I would be left at home alone. That makes a kid grow up in a hurry!

During my youth I lived in Hawaii, New York, and Texas. Often I lived in affluent settings. I had everything a child could want except love. Gradually I developed a very cynical, hardened attitude, and I began to create a lot of trouble in school. For awhile my mother put me in a military school. There I was disciplined and had some absolutes, so I straightened out. But as soon as I was out, I was like a dog let out of a cage—I was ready to make up for lost time.

The one ray of light in the midst of all this darkness was the time I spent living with my grandparents. My grandmother told me about Jesus Christ and took me to church. I remember liking that experience, though I didn't understand what was happening. My grandmother had a picture of Jesus on the wall, and I often looked at it for long periods of time, thinking how much I would have enjoyed meeting this Person. He seemed like a very good man to me.

Then the sixties rolled around and the drug movement began to gain momentum. Like so many teenagers in my generation, I was caught up in the music of the time, especially the Beatles. When they released their album "Sergeant Pepper's Lonely Hearts Club Band," we were beginning to "turn on," "tune in," and "drop out," as we said at that time.

A lot of kids took drugs recreationally, just to have fun. I took drugs for a different reason. I was told that they would open my mind and expand my perception, that I would become more aware. My reason for taking drugs was to find some answers and shed my skin of cynicism and hardness. I wanted to become a more caring and loving person.

The first few times I took drugs, I must honestly admit that it was both fun and exciting. But that excitement quickly turned sour. I started by smoking marijuana on the weekends. Soon it was every day. Then smoking marijuana once a day wasn't enough. It became twice a day, then three times. At school I ran around with a group known as "potheads."

About this time I transferred to Newport Harbor High School, where I decided to change my identity. Up till now I was a rather clean-cut kid—button-down collar and relatively neatly dressed. But now I let my hair grow long. I started wearing ratty, beat-up clothes and hanging out with the "dopers." Our idea of a good time was to get loaded at lunch, then sit around on the front lawn, eat, and laugh because we thought we were cooler than everybody else.

Soon marijuana wasn't doing it for me anymore. I heard that LSD was the "ultimate trip," and I took it a number of times. One time I overdosed and started hearing a voice over and over in my head saying, "You are going to die. You are going to die." I walked into the bathroom and looked in the mirror and saw a skeleton where my face should have been.

I was terrified. I began to call out to God, really hoping there was some way out of this trap. After I came down from that trip I was more careful. But occasionally I would have a flashback, and the hallucination would occur again when I smoked marijuana.

God used a number of things to penetrate my shell. One was a group on campus that we unaffectionately called "Jesus freaks." A lot of them looked somewhat like I did: They had long hair, but they carried Bibles and were always smiling. In fact, some of them were people with whom I used to get stoned. That confused me. I could understand someone being this way if he had grown up in church, but it didn't make sense that someone could become this way overnight. So I kept an eye on this group of Christians.

One night I went to a movie that is now a classic—Ben Hur. Though it was a Hollywood production, it had a message for me. When I saw the depiction of Jesus dying on the cross, I cried. I didn't know He was God at the time, but I knew He was very good, and it seemed tragic that His life was taken from Him. After the movie "Jesus freaks" were waiting outside the theater, and one of them came up and told me more about Jesus. I took his booklet and added it to my collection.

Soon afterward a pretty girl caught my eye at school and I fell in love with her. I was often kidded because I was infatuated with girls before I'd even met them. But there was something different about this one. The only way I can explain it is to say that it was like she had a light inside her. One day I saw her talking with a friend of mine, so I walked over, hoping for an introduction. In her arms were several books, and I noticed that one of them had black leather covers, gold-edged pages, and a ribbon hanging out—the Bible. "What a waste!" I thought. "She's a Jesus freak." Nevertheless, the girl continued to fascinate me.

At that time Newport Harbor High School had a lot of Christians on campus. During lunch hour they would meet on the front lawn, sing songs about God, and have Bible studies. My friends and I would laugh at them. One Friday during lunch I received a tip about a guy on campus who was selling really good LSD. With the weekend just around the corner, I wanted to "score some," as we would say. As I was walking across campus looking for the guy, I walked past the Jesus freaks singing on the lawn, and there was that girl. "What is with them?" I wondered. "Why do they act that way?" On impulse I decided to sit down and lis-ten—though not too close; I didn't want my friends to think I'd joined up. (That would have been social suicide.) But I figured if I could hear what they believed, enough to tell this girl I believed it, then I might get to know her better.

They sang a number of simple melodic songs about their God, and I couldn't help but notice the joy they seemed to have. Then a bearded, long-haired guy stood up and began to teach from the Bible. I had never heard preaching like this before—or if I had, it had not penetrated. One state-ment he made was like a lightning bolt from heaven right to my heart: "Jesus said, 'You're either for me or against me; you're either with me or you are in opposition to me.' " At that moment I realized I was not a Christian, for I was definitely not for Jesus. I looked around at these people and saw that they had something I surely did not have.

The speaker continued, "If you want to make a commit-ment to Jesus Christ, get up and come forward right now." High school students started getting up and walking for-ward to pray in front of everyone. I hung my head and thought, "I'd really like to do that, but there is no way possible. I could never do it." Yet a moment later I was up front praying; I don't know how I got there. As soon as the prayer was over, the school bell unceremoniously rang and we were dismissed to fifth period.

Something wonderful happened that lunch hour, but for a while I wasn't sure what it was. The girl I had been tracking came up and threw her arms around me and said, "Praise the Lord, brother!" I liked that. Unfortunately, nobody explained what it meant to follow Christ now that I was with Him.

I went ahead with my plans for the weekend. Several of my friends and I headed to the hills to take some acid and "trip out on nature." They began taking LSD and offered me some. Suddenly I realized I didn't want it. It was repulsive. "No, I'm just going to go smoke instead," I said. I took my little lid of marijuana and my pipe and went and sat on a rock overlooking a spectacular view. As I sat, I realized that it seemed a little prettier and a little more vibrant than it ever had before. As I began to stuff my pipe with marijuana, I seemed to hear a voice saying, "You don't need that anymore." I knew it was God speaking to me, and I replied, "God, if You are really there, if You can really change me, I'll give You the chance right now." I stood up and threw the pipe and marijuana down the side of the hill.

Well, God was faithful. Despite my doubts, He changed me. I spent time with the Christians and began to do what they said was important for my spiritual growth. I bought a Bible and began to read it, and it was as though God was speaking directly to me. I began to put the principles of the Bible into practice. Prayer became a wonderful experience; I felt like God was really hearing me. When He began to answer my prayers, it made me more confident of what He had done in my life. Then I began to attend church and found many other people who loved the Lord.

The reason my life began to radically change was because I heard the gospel, and it wasn't watered down. I believe that today's young people (and each generation following) need the same undiluted gospel. In the church I pastor we have approximately 2500 people in our Sunday evening service, and frequently half of them are teenagers. We teach in-depth Bible studies and challenge the people to come to Jesus Christ and be His disciples. Every week we

see between 50 and 100 people make that commitment—
and many of them are teenagers!

If you have a void in your life, a void you've tried to fill by
taking drugs, getting drunk, or other diversions, you need
to know that Jesus offers you fulfillment. He says that if
you come to Him, you can drink living water (John 4:14).
The Bible says that only Jesus can satisfy the thirst of your
soul. Only He can fill that void in your life; drugs, sexual
promiscuity, religion, or any other thing cannot fill it. If
you are a person with no direction in life, so that you are
influenced by your peers into making wrong decisions,
Jesus offers you a purpose and an individual plan for your
life. He has given you a book of absolutes to live by—the
Bible. You can know what is right. You can know what is
wrong. You can know what to do and when to do it.

One of the most exciting discoveries I made when I first
became a Christian was that God had a plan for *me*, for Greg
Laurie, that was unlike His plan for anyone else. I was not
just another person cut out of the same cookie-cutter mold.
God wasn't making me into a clone of someone else. I was
an individual. He came to me at a level where I could relate
to Him, and then He started showing me His plan for my
life.

That is why when I say "You need to have an encounter
with Jesus Christ," I don't mean that you just need to
believe there is a God, or that you have to go to church
because your parents want you to. You need to fully commit your life to Christ. I know that some of you reading this
have been involved with drugs. Perhaps you have not yet
made a commitment to Christ. There are others who have
been brought up in a Christian home. You've had the Bible
taught to you as a child. You may even think, "I need to go
out and taste what this world has to offer before I can fully
appreciate Jesus Christ." Don't believe that! It's a lie from
the devil himself. If you were brought up in a Christian
home and never got diverted into drugs or immorality,
thank God for it and follow Him with fervency.

Jesus said, "The thief does not come except to steal, and to kill, and to destroy. I have come that they may have life, and that they may have it more abundantly" (John 10:10). That's the best contrast I can give you as to your choices in life. You are either going to follow Jesus Christ or you are going to follow Satan.

You may think that you won't follow Satan or Jesus, that somehow you'll be the master of your own destiny. You'd better WISE UP! The Bible says you're a captive of Satan unless you've surrendered to Jesus. Who do you think is the Pied Piper to the crowd that is going the wrong direction? Is it just a coincidence that so many young people are into drugs, loose sex, and alcoholism? It's *not* a coincidence. Satan is the mastermind, and his greatest deception is making people think he doesn't even exist. He masquerades in our society as some character with a red suit, long tail, and pitchfork. But the Bible describes him as an angel of light, a powerful force that, if he were to appear, could *seem* like a messenger from God Himself. He is able to persuade. He is an incredible liar. That's why he is able to deceive so many people—because he's real. He makes people think they are in control when in reality he pulls the strings as efficiently as any master puppeteer.

Satan, the thief, comes only to kill and destroy. He hates you. He seeks to wipe out innocent lives through suicide. But Jesus, in contrast, says, "I have come that you might have life, and have it more abundantly." Before I became a Christian, the one thing that appealed to me the most about Christians was not that they claimed to have an eternal destiny in heaven, though that was appealing. Rather, they seemed to enjoy life *now*. They had a dimension of life I had never known before. This is the great contrast of the gospel. When we meet Christ, we literally go from death into life.

We have seen this contrast in the responses from our television program on teen suicide. A 19-year-old called from Arizona. He was crying as he told us how he had gone into his backyard and said, "God, if You are there, you're going to have to show Yourself to me because I'm ready to take my life." He walked back into his house and saw our program. What's amazing is that we did not broadcast our program in Arizona. He had a satellite dish and picked up the program "by accident" as he randomly turned the channels. When he heard this message of life, he called the number and gave his life to the Lord.

You may remember the ferry disaster off the coast of Belgium in 1987. One hero who emerged from this tragedy was a man who put his six-foot-three frame to good use. During the accident there were people sitting in a corner of the sinking vessel who needed to reach the safety of a small island of metal. But the space was too large for people to jump across. So this tall man stretched his frame across the gap and became a human bridge. Twenty people crossed over this man to safety. His heroic deed was literally life-saving because, as one survivor commented later, "Otherwise we couldn't have crossed the space."

That's our dilemma in reaching God. We, by ourselves, can't "cross the space." So God became that bridge for us when He sent Jesus Christ to this earth to die on the cross and rise again from the dead. He bore all of our sins on Himself so that we could enter into a relationship with God.

When we receive Christ into our life ("As many as *received* Him, to them He gave the right to become children of God"—John 1:12), we begin to be transformed into God's image. He cleanses us of our sins and changes our nature and desires. He instills His Holy Spirit into our lives and gives us a calling to serve Him in some special way.

Because God lives inside me, I now have something to live for! I have a purpose, a vision for living. I actually began preaching when I was still a teenager—just 19 years old. Over the years I have not altered my message, and with every new group of teens I face, I still find a hunger for answers and a desire to hear and live up to the challenges of the gospel.

Maybe you're not a teenager, yet have contemplated suicide or even attempted it. Maybe you've never gone that far, but you know what it feels like to be lonely. You know how it feels to be isolated. You understand that feeling of hopelessness. Or perhaps you *are* a teenager and you've always been a good kid, and you've never even thought about suicide. Wherever you are, whatever your state, everybody needs Jesus Christ—young or old, religious or nonreligious, rich or poor, educated or illiterate. We all need God because God created us with a void in our lives that only He can fill. Jesus said, "I stand at the door and knock. If anyone hears My voice and opens the door, I will come in . . ." (Revelation 3:20).

Even as you are reading these words right now, you are going to cast a vote. Jesus said that we are either for Him or against Him (Matthew 12:30). We all have to make a decision to say either "yes" or "no" to God. What's your decision? Some would say, "I'm not going to do either. I'm going to be neutral." That's not an option. To try to find neutral ground is to choose against God. Might I suggest that if you've never made a decision to let Jesus into your life, do so right now. It's the *only* real way to end the pain.

If you've never asked Christ to come into your life and forgive you of your sins, bow your head and do so right now in prayer.

All We Like Sheep

6

All We Like Sheep

Studies have shown that the need for acceptance in a group is one of the most powerful forces molding the minds of young people today. A recent poll taken by *Teen-Age* magazine revealed that out of 337 respondents, 90 percent admitted to feeling peer pressure, and 80 percent said they gave into that pressure at least once a week, even when they knew they were doing wrong. On top of that, 60 percent admitted to pressuring others while only half said they tried to stop peer pressure. We certainly must not underestimate the power of peer pressure, and as Christians we must provide direction and help in this area.

Frances doesn't come from a broken home, but her relationship with her mother is a constant battle. When she was 15, Frances tried to slash her wrists after one of their fights. Her mother found her before she got very far, and they had another verbal battle. Frances' brother was a Christian, and he arranged for an older Christian woman to call his sister and befriend her. That woman led Frances to the Lord, and for two years she was involved in a Christian program at her high school.

During the summer following her junior year, Frances slipped back into her old life. "There was no Bible study during the summer," she explains, "and everyone was going away. So I started hanging around with my old friends. I fell back into alcohol, and I was drinking every day."

Part of the problem was that Frances forgot the kind of crowd she had been a part of. "Drugs, alcohol, sex—they were doing everything," she says. "Everybody was in a different car and doing different drugs, and you would go around and switch cars. Your friends were telling you, 'If you won't do this, you're not part of us. You can't be our friend. You can't hang around us because you're cramping our style.' You're very conscious of it, and it can break you."

That type of living plus more fights with her mother led Frances to another suicide attempt before her Christian friends came to the rescue and gave her the support she needed to straighten out her life.

Obviously, peer pressure is a major contributing factor to this problem of teenage suicide, and it is compounded by the high divorce rate and the breakdown of the family unit. Unfortunately, one reinforces the other. Often there is no father or mother in the home for an adolescent to talk to when he's facing these enormous pressures. Even when both parents are home, straight talk between a parent and child is rare. As we've seen, kids will turn to music, drugs, friends, and even video games before going to Mom and Dad.

Lance, the young man in chapter 4 whose parents were divorced, desperately wanted friends. "There's this feeling inside of you that you just have to belong," he says. "You don't want people to look at you and laugh and make jokes about you. I've always been kind of a loner, and I'd do anything to belong. That's why I started swearing and smoking pot and drinking. It's coming to the point today where you have to do some drastic things to get friends, and that's not right."

An interesting study by a group of doctors is recorded in *Preparing for Adolescence*, by Dr. James Dobson. An experiment was conducted to evaluate how group pressure influences young people. Groups of ten teenagers were invited into a room and told that they were going to be tested for their perception to determine how well each student could see the front of the room. In reality, all of the teenagers were very close to the front and could see easily. The doctors then held up cards in the front of the room. On each card were three lines labeled "A," "B," and "C." Each line was a different length. Each time one of the doctors pointed to the longest line on one of the cards, the teens were instructed to raise their hands. However, nine of the ten students in each group were instructed to knowingly vote for the wrong line every time. Even though one line was longer than the others, nine agreed to say it was shorter. So only one student was voting for what he actually saw, not knowing he was the guinea pig.

As the first card was held up and the doctor pointed to line A, which was obviously shorter than line B, all nine students cooperating in the experiment raised their hands. The student being tested looked up in disbelief, knowing that line B was the longest. Still, he voted with the rest, later admitting that he thought he must have missed the directions. Even when the directions were restated, the lone person continued to vote for the shorter lines along with the group. In 75 percent of the groups, the results were the same: The young people being tested voted time after time against what they *knew* was true. They simply did not want to stand out. Interestingly, if just one other student among the nine voted for the correct line, then chances were greatly improved that the student being tested would also vote for what he thought was right. The implication is clear: Courage to take a stand comes easier when someone else will stand with you.[1]

This same kind of pressure is hurting a lot of Christian young people today, keeping them from standing up and being counted as followers of Jesus Christ. Many of today's Christian teens have developed a chameleon-like nature. When they come to church they act like Christians, but when they are around nonbelieving friends they act like everybody else. Christianity has become a charade. We obviously need young people who will stand up and be counted, even though everyone else may be going the other way. But how can we help them do so?

The Bible has a good description of peer pressure, using the metaphor of sheep: "All we like sheep have gone astray; we have turned, every one, to his own way" (Isaiah 53:6). Of all the animals God could have compared us to, it is noteworthy that He picked sheep because sheep are really quite stupid. Phillip Keller in his books *A Shepherd Looks at Psalm 23* and *The Good Shepherd* describes many of the characteristics of sheep. In his writings he explains that sheep tend to want to stick together. They are afraid to stand out. In fact, some sheep are so timid and fearful that an entire flock can be panicked into a stampede by one stray jackrabbit jumping from the bushes. When one startled sheep runs, the others follow in blind fear, bumping and bruising themselves and even breaking their legs in the excitement.

Not long ago I heard a news report describing how two stray dogs stampeded some 200 sheep over a cliff. Keller describes how entire flocks of sheep have been known to go one after another over the side of a cliff, following one greedy sheep that passed the point of no return while stretching for a morsel of grass. Undaunted by the failure of the first sheep, the others will follow blindly.

Slaughterhouses take advantage of this trait in sheep. They'll train what they call a "Judas goat" to lead the sheep up a long ramp to the room where they will be butchered. All they have to do is get that "Judas goat" up the ramp, and all the others will follow him. At the last moment a side door opens, freeing the "Judas goat" so he can once again practice his deception while the rest go blindly to their demise.

Keller also noted that sheep, when confronted by a predator such as a mountain lion or bear, will at times just stand

and watch, as if oblivious to the danger, while the predator will take one sheep after another and tear it limb from limb. Somehow they pretend that there is no danger.

Aren't we just like sheep! We have all heard stories of people being beaten or robbed in the streets of our cities while crowds of people stand around and act like nothing is wrong. And how many teenagers today are watching their friends "go over the cliff" by overdosing on drugs? It doesn't seem to deter those people who are involved with drugs. In fact, it seems to make them heroes. Jim Morrison, Janice Joplin, and Jimmy Hendrix all died drug-related deaths; they're now heroes to many young people.

Something is wrong when we idolize and make role models out of people like this. People who destroyed their lives should stand instead as examples of what happens when we play around with sin. You would think that after seeing so many drug overdoses, or seeing how many un-wed teens get pregnant, today's youth might understand that it can happen to them just as easily. Yet the prevailing sentiment is "That won't happen to me. I'll be the *one* person it won't happen to." What a shock it is when it does happen!

A recent study reported in *USA Today* illustrates this truth. The study shows that fear is not an effective deter-rent to teen drug use. In fact, kids who turn down drugs base their choice on their self-image and not on school drug programs. So drug education that emphasizes health dan-gers and legal risks may be missing the mark. What this report shows is the need for clear moral values. It's been proven time and again that a young person doesn't turn from drugs or sex or anything else because he's afraid of the consequences.

Many people today just go along with whatever is sup-posedly "cool." What I want to know is, exactly what is "cool"? Who determines what colors and styles are out and in? Who determines what kind of music is out or in? Who determines what's hot and what's not? No one seems to know, yet we blindly follow year after year. The crazy thing is that things *never* really change. Most of the styles are just a rehashing of old styles we've seen before. And in any given year there are always those we call "rebels." They never change either; it's interesting that they always dress alike. There is actually a "conformity" to being a non-conformist. Indeed, all we like sheep have gone astray! Most of us just get in line and do what everyone else does. The only way to break free from the crowd, to escape from the flock that is heading toward destruction, is to follow the Good Shepherd, Jesus Christ!

Jesus said that His sheep will follow the Good Shepherd, for they know His voice (John 10:14-16). If you really want to follow Jesus Christ you will do so, and if you do not follow Him you will be a stray. The word "follow" implies more than just the thought of a sheep tagging along blindly behind its owner. It speaks of a deliberate decision based on specific instruction. It's a choice we can make. As the old hymn puts it, "I have decided to follow Jesus. Though none come with me, still I will follow. I have decided to follow Jesus." Following Jesus is a choice we make, just as we choose our friends.

The apostle Paul told young Timothy to "flee also youthful lusts; but pursue righteousness, faith, love, peace *with those who call on the Lord out of a pure heart*" (2 Timothy 2:22).

There is an important consideration when choosing the people with whom you'll hang around: Forming good solid friendships built on a foundation of God's Word is one of the surest methods of combating peer pressure. Just as Dr. Dobson's study on peer pressure demonstrated, having even one other person with you makes taking a stand much easier. But a lot of Christians hang around with people who are not Christians, at the expense of making Christian friends. Though we want to reach those who are lost, we must be careful not to be dragged into sin because we isolate ourselves with people in the world.

There is another aspect of sheep and shepherding that I think parallels the problem of peer pressure and offers a solution. When sheep are scattered along the countryside, the strays tend to graze where they choose. Shepherds in the Far East have a fascinating way of getting these sheep to come home. Every shepherd will have a small group of sheep that are especially attached to him. They are like pets. They love to be next to him; in fact sometimes they become a nuisance because he can't get them out from under his feet. When it's time to head for home, the shepherd places his pet sheep in the midst of the scattered flock. Then as he heads for home, his pet sheep follow and the strays naturally follow along with them.

I see a parallel here. We need young people today who are so in love with Jesus that they lead others closer to Him. These young people will stand up for God and do what is right regardless of what others are saying and doing. These young people will love to be around Jesus, the Good Shepherd, and in the process they will naturally lead others to Him. This is what drew me to Christ. May God help you to be such a person!

Dealing with
Peer Pressure

7

Dealing with Peer Pressure

It is certainly important to define peer pressure and acknowledge its strong pull on today's young people. But it would be a tremendous waste of time and paper to talk about the dilemma of peer pressure and its role in teenage suicide without giving good, solid biblical advice on how to cope with these pressures. That's why God has given us His written plan, within which we can find answers and guidelines to all of life's difficulties and problems. When it comes to peer presure, I can't think of a more direct and useful story than that of Shadrach, Meshach, and Abednego.

These three young Hebrews appear in the book of Daniel, chapters 2 and 3. Nebuchadnezzar was the ruling king of Babylon, the most powerful nation on earth. One night Nebuchadnezzar had a very strange dream in which he saw a giant statue or image that had a head of gold, breast and arms of silver, belly and thighs of brass, legs of iron, and feet of iron and clay. The king called together his religious experts, astrologers, and wise men (so called) and ordered them to tell him what he had dreamed, and the meaning of the dream. Of course they couldn't do so. When Daniel heard about the problem, he offered to help and asked his three friends—Shadrach, Meshach, and Abednego—to pray that God would reveal this mystery to him. God did so. Then Daniel went to Nebuchadnezzar and revealed a prophetic preview of world history represented in the statue's head of gold, breast and arms of silver, thighs of brass, and legs and feet of iron and clay. These represented the various Gentile kingdoms that would rule upon the earth right up to the time of the return of Jesus Christ. From our twentieth-century perspective we can now look back and see just how each of those nations came into being. It's a fascinating story, but that is not the point of our study.

Nebuchadnezzar's kingdom of Babylon, represented by the head of gold, was at the very top of the image in his dream. Such an honor was more than his pride and ego could stand, and sometime later he thought, "If the head of gold represented Babylon, and I'm the head of Babylon, then I'll make a statue out of gold from top to bottom." We don't know for sure who the statue looked like, but I think it might have been Nebuchadnezzar. He formed this statue to stand some 90 feet tall and nine feet wide. Then he sent word to all of Babylon, which was a very large nation with many provinces, that he wanted representatives from every township and city to have representatives at the dedication of this image. Thousands of people gathered on the plain of Dura, where the statue was erected. I don't know if these people knew what they were getting into, but Nebuchadnezzar ordered that when the music began, everyone was to bow down before the image. It wasn't an option, either, for he told them that anybody who refused would be given a front-row seat in the fiery furnace. It was clearly easier to bow under the circumstances, especially since *everybody else was doing it*.

In my mind I can see this mass of humanity waiting for the music to play. Then, in the midst of all the excitment, everyone bows—except for three Hebrew teenagers. I can see them standing defiantly against the king's command, refusing to bow amid thousands of others with lesser conviction. You see, they had one small problem. God had told these young men through Scripture, *"You shall have no other*

gods before Me. You shall not make for yourself any carved image"
(Exodus 20:3,4). This caused them to stand up and say, "We
can't bow; it's against what we believe." They were facing
peer pressure of a sort that we will probably never see.

Soon word got to Nebuchadnezzar concerning these
three young government leaders. They had positions that
included power and money, and for them not to bow was to
throw it all away. But to them, bowing meant throwing
away their integrity and their commitment to God. Years
later, when Jesus walked this earth, He defined it this way,
"What will it profit a man if he gains the whole world and
loses his own soul?" (Mark 8:36).

In a rage at their disobedience, Nebuchadnezzar gave
the command to bring Shadrach, Meshach, and Abednego
before him. Nebuchadnezzar spoke to them and said, "Is it
true, Shadrach, Meshach, and Abednego, that you do not
serve my gods or worship the gold image that I have set up?
Now if you are ready at the time you hear the sound of
[music to] fall down and worship the image which I have
made, good! But if you do not worship, you will be cast
immediately into the midst of a burning fiery furnace."
Then he gave a direct challenge to the God they believed in,
saying, "And who is the god who will deliver you from my
hands?" (Daniel 3:14,15). In effect, he was daring God.
Now this is not something that any mere mortal should do!
Apparently Nebuchadnezzar hadn't come to the realiza-
tion that "his arms were too short to box with God." It
reminds me of a statement made by another fool, Egypt's
Pharaoh, when he said to Moses, "Who is the Lord, that I
should obey His voice?" (Exodus 5:2). He found out when
he got a permanent bath in the Red Sea!

Now imagine you are Shadrach, Meshach, or Abednego,
and everybody else is bowing before the statue. King Nebu-
uchadnezzar has decided to give you a second chance. It
would be very tempting to justify your position by saying,
"Maybe God is letting me off the hook. If I just go along

with the crowd, I can cross my fingers behind my back and bow with everybody, then repent and ask the Lord to forgive me." Or a compromise could be reached by adopting that philosophy of "When in Babylon, do as the Babylonians do." Another logical justification would be to think "If we don't bow we'll be dead, and what good are we to God if we are dead!" But the simple fact is that God had said, "Don't ever bow." Would you have done the same as these three young men?

Notice the immediate response of these three faithful followers: "Nebuchadnezzar, we have no need to answer you in this matter" (verse 16). They said there wasn't anything to discuss. And in the following verse comes one of the boldest and most trusting statements ever made by any of God's children: "If that is the case, our God whom we serve is able to deliver us from the burning fiery furnace and He will deliver us from your hand, O king. But if not, let it be known to you, O king, that we do not serve your god, nor will we worship the gold image which you have set up." In essence, they concluded that it would be better to burn for a few short minutes in the furnace of Nebuchadnezzar than to disobey God and suffer the consequences.

These three heroes are not alone in church history with their daring stand. I think, for example, of Polycarp, a highly respected church leader who lived during the first and second centuries. As an old man he was brought before the Roman proconsul in the amphitheater and ordered to stop proclaiming the gospel. He was told that if he would "swear by the genius of Caesar" he would be spared. Freedom was his if he would simply say "Caesar is Lord." There stood Polycarp. At 86 years of age he could have bowed to Caesar and perhaps gained a few more years to preach the gospel. This was his reply: "Eighty-six years have I served Him. He has done me no wrong. How can I blaspheme my King who saved me?" While taking him to the stake to be burned, the guard who was to torch him said, "I don't want to burn you, old man. The fire will be hot." But Polycarp replied, "Not as hot as the fire that they will experience who reject my Lord Jesus Christ." He was tied to the stake and the fire was lit. The flames encircled him but did not touch him as he began to sing praises to God. One of the Roman soldiers standing nearby then took a spear and lanced Polycarp with it, and his blood extinguished the flames of the fire. I'm sure the echo of that final statement, "It's not as hot as the fire that they will experience who reject my Lord Jesus Christ," sounded in the ears of those soldiers for many years to come.

Polycarp grabbed hold of a promise that not many Christians today are willing to stand on. It says, "All who desire to live godly in Christ Jesus will suffer persecution" (2 Timothy 3:12). I often hear people claim a promise of God's supernatural provision, or perhaps a promise of healing, but very infrequently do I hear someone say, "Lord, you promised I'd be persecuted; let's have it!" Perhaps the reason we've not persecuted today is because we're not living godly lives. Then there are those who say they *are* persecuted, but I wonder if it's not for the wrong reasons. Many times Christians are persecuted not for godly living but for being obnoxious, condemning, or simply idiotic. God help us to be persecuted for righteousness and because we are like Jesus Christ!

Jesus said that the world hated Him and that it would hate us too. It's as simple as that. Being a Christian in a dark world is like a light shining in a dark place, or like salt rubbed in an open wound. In some countries in this world today, people are still put to death for their faith in Jesus Christ. They are following in the example of Shadrach, Meshach, and Abednego. They have believed, "Our God is able."

Needless to say, Nebuchadnezzar was not real excited about that response. The anger showed in the expression on his face, and he commanded that the furnace be heated

seven times hotter than normal. Now the *fire* may have
been *hot*, but *Nebuchadnezzar* was even *hotter*. He commanded
certain mighty men of valor who were in his army to bind
Shadrach, Meshach, and Abednego and cast them into the
burning fiery furnace still dressed in their coats, pants,
turbans, and other garments. The fire was so hot and
Nebuchadnezzar's command so urgent that the men who
took Shadrach, Meshach, and Abednego to the mouth of
the furnace died from the intense heat. It's interesting that
the very death that was planned for the accused was suffered by the executioners! Nonetheless, Nebuchadnezzar
must have felt confident that he had removed three disobe-
dient Hebrews from his kingdom. But then, to his aston-
ishment, we are told that he rose in haste and said to his
counselors, "Did we not cast three men bound into the
midst of the fire?" They replied, "True, O king." Nebu
chadnezzar, full of fear and amazement, exclaimed, "Look! I
see four men loose, walking in the midst of the fire; and
they are not hurt, and the form of the fourth is like the Son
of God." Guess who was taking a stroll on a Sunday after
noon with Shadrach, Meshach, and Abednego? It was
none other than Jesus Himself!

To do justice to the translation we must understand what
Nebuchadnezzar really said: "There is one who looks like
one of the gods." Nebuchadnezzar was not perceptive
enough to know that he was seeing the one and only true
Son of God, Jesus. I believe this has great significance for
us as Christians today. You see, Jesus does not promise to
always take our problems away, but He does promise to be
with us in the midst of them. As I've already pointed out,
this is repeated in Hebrews 13:5,6, where we are told that
He will never leave us or forsake us, "so we may boldly say:
'The Lord is my helper; I will not fear. What can man do to
me?' " What great confidence we should have! What great
courage should be ours, knowing that we are never alone!

In a classroom situation where people are openly making
light of the God you love, you've got the Lord there with

you, so stand up and be counted! Think of young David when he was down in the valley of Elah and all of Israel was paralyzed by fear because of the boasting, loudmouthed, nine-foot-six Philistine, Goliath, who was looking for someone who had the courage to come down and face him. David wasn't alone in that valley. Though everyone else feared, David knew that God was with him, and one with God is a majority. When we can lay hold of the truth that He is with us, it will change the way we live. Believing that He is really with us allows us to act on His strength, to stand up and be counted, to "be strong in the Lord and in the power of His might" (Ephesians 6:10).

At this point Nebuchadnezzar changed his approach. After all, anyone who could walk around in a furnace and not get burned is worth being nice to! In verse 26 he gives a classic response, which if paraphrased must have sounded something like this:

"Excuse me, Shadrach, Meshach, and Abednego, servants of the Most High God. Come out here, *please*. I hope I didn't offend you. I really didn't mean it. Won't you please come out? How nice to see you again!" At this point Shadrach, Meshach, and Abednego came out from the fire, and all of the governers and counselors crowded around to see these men on whose bodies the fire had no power. Not even the hair on their head was singed, nor were their garments affected. In fact, there wasn't even the smell of fire on them. God had delivered them not just from the fiery furnace, but from within it! To this Nebuchadezzar remarked, "Blessed be the God of Shadrach, Meshach, and Abednego, who sent His Angel and delivered His servants who trusted in Him, and they have frustrated the king's word, and yielded their bodies that they should not serve nor worship any god except their own God!" (verse 28).

What a great testimony to the power of the living God! I think people who are not Christians, though they may poke fun at a person's faith, have greater respect for a

Christian when he stands up for what he believes. Yet many times we think the way to reach people is to be like them. To a certain point that's true—we have to relate to people. The apostle Paul said he desired to "become all things to all men, that I might by all means save some." But this doesn't mean that I have to get down and *do* the things that people are doing to reach them. In the eyes of the world, Shadrach, Meshach, and Abednego were fools, but in their silent stand against compromise they preached volumes about the nature of their God.

Nebuchadnezzar was actually brought to a point of belief because these three Hebrews stood their ground. Today God still employs the "foolishness of preaching" to save those who will believe.

Back in the times of the early church literally millions of men, women, and children were put to death for their faith in Jesus Christ. Some of these martyrs were fed to the lions in the amphitheaters of Rome. Many were crucified, some were covered with animal skins and fed to wild dogs, some were pulled apart on Roman racks. Nero, one of the Caesars, had Christians covered with pitch and lit on fire to act as human torches while he rode through his garden in his chariot, laughing with glee. I might point out that there weren't many halfhearted, fence-walking believers in those days. What advantage would there be to playing Christian or playing church? Either you were a follower of Jesus, willing to lose your life, or you were not.

Sometimes I wonder if it wouldn't be a valid prayer to ask God to send persecution to the church in America. I don't necessarily want persecution in my life, and I don't go around looking for trouble. I don't desire to see other Christians harassed or hurt. However, if that would force us to be the kind of people we need to be as followers of Jesus, maybe it wouldn't be such a bad thing.

We need to either get in line or get out. We must decide what we're going to do and what we're all about. Are we going to follow Jesus because Mom and Dad tell us to, or because there's a great social climate at church, or because we like the music? We need to be followers of Jesus who will stand up and be counted—followers who won't give in as Pontius Pilate did to the crowd that chanted "CRUCIFY HIM!"

It's interesting to notice what Nebuchadnezzar said of Shadrach, Meshach, and Abednego: "They have yielded their bodies that they should not serve or worship any god except their own God." That's what we need to do; we need to yield ourselves to God. In fact this word "yield" is a word that embraces the thought of presenting oneself voluntarily without any restraint. That's what God wants of you. God isn't going to force you to yield yourself to Him. He's not going to threaten you. He's going to ask you because He loves you. He's your loving heavenly Father and He wants you to come of your own will. God created us with that ability to choose to either follow Him or reject Him. The only effective method of dealing with peer pressure is to yield to the power of the Holy Spirit and take a stand for Christ.

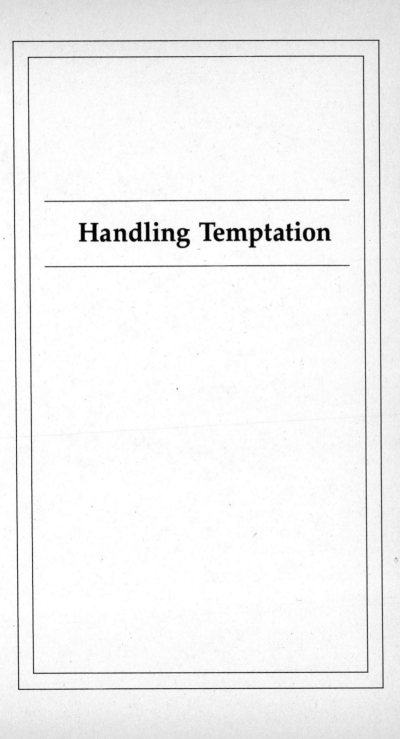

Handling Temptation

8

Handling Temptation

Oscar Wilde once said, "I can resist anything but temptation." That's a sentiment that seems to be echoed by today's youth. Handling temptations incorrectly can destroy the spiritual life of teenage Christians and can further ensnare those young people who have yet to find Christ. But there are certain principles laid out in God's Word to help us deal with temptation when it comes knocking at our door.

For teenagers, suicide is the ultimate temptation. It is Satan's invitation to death. But before it is delivered, it is preceded by a series of other temptations, all designed to bring about the final destruction of a person's soul. Learning how to turn down that final temptation comes with knowing how to live with our adversary's *daily* enticements. If there is any one common temptation facing all of today's teens, one that is a worthy battlefield for learning to say "no" to Satan, it would have to be the area of sex. Though the methods, degrees, and types of temptation may vary, the principles for overcoming sexual temptations remain the same. For the purpose of examining these biblical principles, let's focus on the serious problem of sexual temptation.

Sexual Temptation

One reason there is so much confusion about sex today is that those who should be addressing it are not and those who shouldn't be are. Many kids get their sexual values from TV (sitcoms, soap operas, music videos, and movies). Another major source of information is a young person's peer group. Meanwhile, the church doesn't want to talk about the issue, finding it awkward and uncomfortable. Yet God created sex, and God created the sexual drive, so we had better understand His intention for it.

God has clearly laid down the boundaries in which sex can take place. The only place He has given us sexual freedom is within the marriage relationship. That is the only true "safe sex." Sending a clear message to our youth and to the world concerning God's plan for sex and marriage is the church's responsibility. It bears repeating that God's solution to today's sexual maladies is not birth control but *self*-control.

Our nation faces a serious problem. The United States leads developed nations in its rate of teenage pregnancies, with 96 teenage pregnancies per 1000 girls in the age group of 15 to 19.[1] Most of these teenage girls are unmarried. This is more than double the rate of England, Canada, France, or Sweden. Our country is the only Western nation where teen pregnancy is actually increasing. In addition, an alarming trend is beginning to take place on our high school campuses with so called "school-based health clinics." Within these clinics teens can obtain contraceptives without the permission of a parent. Abortion referral is also given. Proponents use the logic that young people are going to have sex anyway, so it's best to provide protection. Yet studies reveal that young people who use contraceptives simply increase their sexual activity, giving a false sense of freedom that they are without risk and that it is okay to engage in premarital sex. Furthermore, a recent study found that as sexual activity among teens increases, the probability of pregnancy also increases, even when contraceptives are used consistently![2] It is this type of unbiblical reasoning that has allowed teenage pregnancy to get out of control.

The numbers alone are alarming. Eighty percent of all teenage boys and 70 percent of all teenage girls will have sexual relations before they graduate from high school. This year alone, 1.1 million teenage girls will become pregnant, and 30,000 of them will be under 14 years of age. Of these pregnancies, 400,000 will be aborted while 600,000 of these teenage girls will give birth out of wedlock. Of those that have their babies, 96 percent will keep them, leading to a school dropout rate of some 80 percent, with 70 percent winding up on the welfare roles. Those that marry don't fare much better. A majority will be pregnant again within two years, and 60 percent will be divorced in five years.[3]

The snowball effect of all of this is obvious. Uncontrolled passion and lust lead to sexual relations, which often lead to unwanted pregnancies, which many times lead to abortions or unwanted children or marriages that come together out of guilt and duty, often resulting in divorce. The entire cycle is a mockery of God's original plan. We've got to get back to what He has said. He has given us clear directions on how to deal with temptation.

Temptation is nothing new. It goes clear back to the Garden of Eden, when Satan came to Eve. God had put Adam and Eve in the greatest situation possible. He gave them a beautiful garden with only *one* stipulation: "Do not eat from the tree of the knowledge of good and evil." That was it! Here He had given them carte blanche to go anywhere, to enjoy His creation, to enjoy Him for eternity— just stay away from that one tree. So where do we find Eve just "coincidentally" hanging out? You guessed it! At the forbidden tree. It was a choice that was followed by temptation. Just what did she think would happen?

Because Eve was available, Satan enticed and deceived her and got her to eat of that forbidden fruit, then used her as a tool to get Adam, who fell as well. They broke the laws of God and sin entered this world. And in typical fashion, when God confronted Adam and Eve and asked them what had happened, they gave the same excuses that we give today. "It's not my fault," said Adam; "it's the woman's fault." Meanwhile Eve was saying, "The devil made me do it." This was the first passing of the buck, the first attempt to try to justify sin, and it continues today more than ever.

The sad fact is that most temptation we encounter is our own fault because we put ourselves in places where we should not be. In James 1:14,15 we're told, "Each one is tempted when he is drawn away by his own desires and enticed. Then, when desire has conceived, it gives birth to sin; and sin, when it is full-grown, brings forth death."

Many people today, especially in the world of modern psychology and psychiatry, are responding to sin in the same fashion as Adam and Eve. There is a tendency to blame the environment: "It's the fault of my friends"; "it's my parents' fault; I was mistreated as a child"; "it was the girl's fault; she wore revealing clothes"; "it's the pusher's fault; he got me started."

Let's be honest—it's our own evil desires that are enticed in the first place. If there were no craving or desire there would be no temptation. But because those desires are alive in our flesh we naturally face temptation. It's obvious that a dead man can't be tempted. I've never seen a used-car salesman try to make a few sales down at the local cemetery. Why not? Because he'll find no desire there to buy. The same is true for us. If we open ourselves to those areas of temptation where there is a strong desire or craving on our part, then we are simply sitting ducks waiting for the kill.

When James uses the phrase "drawn away by his own desires," the original language actually implies "that combustible material that each person carries within himself." In other words, we're open game for the enemy. The flesh with its selfish desires is the *internal* enemy. Satan with his enticement is the *external* enemy. Jesus said it this way: "From *within*, out of the heart of man, that is what defiles him." It's our own selfish and greedy desires that Satan is going to solicit and tempt. If we are caught up in our own cravings and desires, then we are going to fall to them very easily. In fact the word used by James for "being tempted" carries with it the idea of a juicy worm being dangled before a fish. I can't think of a better way to illustrate temptation; it's that juicy little worm that a fish approaches, looks over, and swims around. Finally he concludes, "Maybe I'll just take one little nibble." But the nibble leads to a bite, which leads to a hook, which leads to being pulled out of the water, which leads to the frying pan. All because Mr. Fish couldn't resist a small nibble! It's not that his desire to eat was wrong—just misplaced. He played and toyed with that desire in the wrong place and at the wrong time! That's why we really have to watch what's going on inside of us.

Now consider this: Satan is the tempter, but God allows temptation in our life, with certain restrictions. *Temptation will always be graded to the fiber of your life.* In other words, God will not let you be tempted or tested above what you are able to bear, as we are told in 1 Corinthians 10:13: "No temptation has overtaken you except such as is common to man; but God is faithful, who will not allow you to be tempted beyond what you are able, but with the temptation will also make the way of escape, that you may be able to bear it." A simple summation would be: God won't give you more than you can handle, and God will not allow the devil to tempt you with something that you do not have the ability to resist. He will put a divine restriction on those things, and there will always be a way out. Sometimes the way out is just rejecting a thought before it starts. Sometimes it's not responding to the invitation to a party, or not becoming involved with a person. In other situations perhaps the only way to get out is to use the two feet that God gave us, and to run! There are times when we must take radical measures to not fall to sin, because the truth is that we often intentionally allow ourselves to face temptation.

One scenario of sexual temptation facing kids today might go like this:

> "I can't believe the temptation my girlfriend and I are facing," says a teenage boy.
>
> "Well, where were you both when you got tempted?" you ask.
>
> "Uh, in my car."
>
> "Where was your car?"
>
> "Parked in a dark alley."
>
> "Do you always park in dark alleys?"
>
> "Well, not usually, but I just wanted to look at the back of some houses, and, well, we were driving along and I thought I would just stop and rest. So then I just said to her, 'Do you mind if I rest my lips on yours for a moment?"
>
> "You said *what*?"
>
> "Well, it was completely innocent. But all of a sudden, you know, her lips were on mine and mine on hers. You know, it just kinda happened. Hey, it wasn't my fault."
>
> "Well, why was that alley dark?"
>
> "I shot the light out earlier in the day with my BB gun."

Obviously this is an exaggerated analogy, but it makes a point.

It's amazing that after all this the perpetrators are actually surprised when the animal instinct kicks in and they sin! Though consciously we hate to admit it, subconsciously we will often plot the entire scheme. And when those desires strike, that combustible material inside of us explodes. We should never be surprised when we fall.

I've heard of men who can't understand why they continually face sexual temptation. Upon closer examination, however, it's not unusual to find that these same men subscribe to pornographic magazines. And when their marriage fails, it's amazing how often God gets the blame! "O God, You let me get tempted above what I am able to bear." The fact of the matter is that most people don't even need outside help with temptation. They simply self-destruct. One person summed it up like this: "Sow a thought, reap an act; sow an act, reap a habit; sow a habit, reap a character; sow a character, reap a destiny." It all starts with those so-called innocent thoughts that we allow to enter our minds. Even as there is a law of gravity that dictates "What goes up must come down," so there is a law of sowing and reaping. God says, "Whatever a man sows, that he will also reap. For he who sows to his flesh will of the flesh reap corruption, but he who sows to the Spirit will of the Spirit reap everlasting life" (Galatians 6:7,8). It's a law of God. It can't be changed. Therefore when you start toying with sin, it eventually will grab hold of you.

David, the author of many of the Psalms, had a somewhat checkered life. He is often remembered for the sin he fell into with a woman named Bathsheba. That was a typical case of failing to deal rightly with temptation, and, as is most often the case, his downfall started with thoughts he toyed with in his mind. Studies have found, and experience affirms, that men are stimulated by what they *see*. Women, on the other hand, are more stimulated by touch and romance. For David, the sight of Bathsheba bathing on her rooftop set the wheels of his imagination turning. It is often said, "It's that second look that gets you in trouble." Such was the case with David. The first look, unfortunately, is oftentimes unavoidable, but it becomes a source of temptation. Sometimes on television we see tempting things put in front of us. Sometimes magazine covers don't leave a whole lot to the imagination. We can't always avoid the first look, but we can sure avoid the second! So when lust comes knocking at your door, may I suggest that you send Jesus Christ to answer it. If the house of your mind is filled with the things of God, there will be no room for impure thoughts.

The Bible speaks of two men who dealt with sexual temptation—one successfully, the other unsuccessfully. Their names were Joseph and Samson, and a look at their stories will give us great insight into overcoming temptation in any form.

Samson

Samson, without a doubt, is one of the greatest paradoxes in history. You might say that he was a "he-man" with a "she weakness." We all know that Samson was filled with incredible supernatural strength. On one occasion when God's Spirit came upon him he killed a lion with his bare hands and on another occasion he killed a thousand of his enemies, the Philistines, with the jawbone of an ass. But even though Samson could kill a thousand Philistines with a jawbone of an ass, he could not control his own passions.

Samson was raised in a good home by godly parents. From his very birth, which was foretold by an angel, he was set apart to the Lord, and one day he became the leader of all Israel. He had every privilege a person could want. But Samson was deceived into thinking he could toy with sin without losing control. Once again I refer to the Scripture that asks the question "Can a man take fire to his bosom and . . . not be burned?" (Proverbs 6:27). If only Samson could have heeded such advice.

Often a parent will warn his child "Don't play with fire," only to have his child end up learning the hard way by burning his fingers. When I was a little kid I used to love to set my little plastic army men on fire. I got some sort of strange pleasure watching them melt into little green blobs. One day when my mother was gone I was burning my army men on top of newspapers. During this little melting routine the newspaper caught on fire. As you might imagine, I panicked, and in doing so I put the flaming paper into the wastebasket, which unfortunately was made of wicker. The next thing I knew, it too was on fire. Believe me, I was scared. Fortunately, I was able to get some water and put the whole mess out before I burned the whole house down. I was just as foolish as Samson. I thought, "I can play with fire. I'm six years old. I know what I'm doing." That's what people think of lust: "I can control it; I'll just get to that one point and then stop." DON'T EVER BELIEVE THAT LIE. It's like lighting the fuse of the bomb. Once ignited, it is very difficult to stop.

As we pick up Samson's story in the book of Judges (16:5) we read, "The lords of the Philistines came up to [Delilah] and said to her, 'Entice him, and find out where his great strength lies, and by what means we may overpower him, that we may bind him to afflict him; and every one of us will give you eleven hundred pieces of silver.' "

Today that would come to about 140,000 dollars. So Delilah said to Samson, "Please tell me where your great strength lies, and with what you may be bound to afflict you." Her forthrightness is nearly beyond belief! But Samson had a real weakness for women, and he was hooked on Delilah, who must have been a real beauty. You would think that Samson would be cautious, but instead he toys with her when he replies, "If they bind me with seven fresh bowstrings not yet dried, then I shall become weak, and be like any other man." So Delilah, working with the lords of the Philistines who were hidden nearby, came up with seven fresh bowstrings not yet dried and bound Samson, who was with her in her room. Once tied, Delilah jumped back from Samson and shouted, "The Philistines are upon you, Samson!" But he broke the bowstrings effortlessly, and the secret of his strength was still unknown.

Then Delilah said to Samson, "Look, you have mocked me and told me lies. Now please tell me what you may be bound with." At this point you would think that Samson would come to his senses. Couldn't he see that this was a trap? No, he couldn't, and the reason is that he thought he was in love but was actually "in lust." It's a symptom we see a lot of today. The lyrics of a song which a friend of mine wrote put it this way: "He gives love for pleasure, she gives pleasure to be loved." Another way to put it is: Men give love to get sex and women give sex to get love.

I think this can be illustrated by some famous "come-on" lines that men use to coerce girls to get sexually involved. Here are a few classics:

"If you really love me, you'll do it."
"Life is so uncertain. Who knows whether we'll be alive tomorrow. It would be a shame if you died in an accident without experiencing the greatest thrill of all."
"I want to marry you someday, and we should first find out if we're sexually compatible."
"I promise you we won't go all the way unless you want to. I'll stop whenever you say."
"I know you want it as much as I do, but you're afraid of your reputation. I swear I'll never tell anyone. It will be our secret."
"It isn't sex I'm after. I'm really in love with you, and if you get pregnant I'll marry you."

That isn't love, that's LUST. Any man who says that sex is the way you prove your love and loyalty is being absurd. Yet this same type of lust was driving Samson. He was hooked. He didn't even realize he had fallen into a trap. He thought he was strong enough to endure anything. Scripture warns of this: "Let him who thinks he stands take heed lest he fall" (1 Corinthians 10:12).

Having escaped Delilah's first attempt, Samson continued dabbling and further deceived her by saying, "If they bind me securely with new ropes that have never been used, then I shall become weak, and be like any other man." Predictably, she did just that, and having bound him she cried out once more, "The Philistines are upon you, Samson!" With his God-given strength still intact he broke the rope like thread. Again Delilah went back to Samson, saying, "Until now you have mocked me and told me lies. Tell me what you may be bound with." Here we find an interesting thing about Samson's reply. He said, "If you weave the seven locks of my head into the web of the loom. . . ." It was another lie concerning the secret of his strength, but notice that now he is getting closer to the truth. Samson's strength was the result of his obedience to the Nazirite vow, which prohibited him from cutting his hair. As long as he remained faithful to that vow, God would grant him supernatural strength. Therefore to cut his hair was an outward symbol representing an inward breaking of God's commandment in his heart. He was weakening to the temptations of Delilah. Toying with sin was beginning to show results. She was getting closer to the truth, though again her effort to rob him of his strength failed.

Delilah's sickeningly sweet reply is found in verse 15: "How can you say 'I love you' when your heart is not with me? You have mocked me these three times, and have not told me where your great strength lies." With these words she pestered him daily, continually pressing him for the answer. Finally he broke down and told her, "No razor has ever come upon my head, for I have been a Nazirite to God from my mother's womb. If I am shaven, then my strength will leave me, and I shall become weak, and be like any other man."

Delilah realized that he was finally telling her the truth, so she sent for the lords of the Philistines, saying, "Come up once more, for he has told me all his heart." They gave her the money and she proceeded to lull Samson to sleep with his head on her knees. In the midst of his sleep she called for a man to shave off the seven locks of his head, and his strength left him. She then woke him with a shout: "The Philistines are upon you, Samson!" As he woke from his sleep Samson said (and this is tragic), "I will go out as before, at other times, and shake myself free!" But he soon discovered that the Lord had departed from him. So the Philistines took him, put out his eyes, and brought him down to Gaza, where they bound him with bronze shackles and chained him to a grinding mill.

The once-mighty man of God no longer had eyes and no longer had a kingdom. He faced the monotony of prison and a ruined life, all because he failed to deal with temptation. Surely God was merciful, allowing Samson's strength to return one final time as he stood before the Philistines in a large hall. He was allowed to topple the two pillars that supported the building, killing thousands of the enemy. But Samson died too. That's the way it is with sin—it brings death, it brings separation from God. There's little doubt that Samson repented of his deeds and found forgiveness, but look at the cost!

How many today are being wiped out by the effects of sin! We've already seen that 600,000 teenagers try to kill themselves each year. That's 600,000 cases of falling to temptation—and 6000 succeed in taking their lives. Or look at the number one killer of teenagers in our country—automobile crashes. In 1981 alone such crashes ended 15,000 young lives. According to the National Safety Council, the primary reason for this enormous death toll is alcohol. It is estimated that an average of 8000 teenage deaths and 40,000 injuries per year are a direct result of drunken driving. And that's a direct result of not being able to deal with temptation properly.

Now that we've seen the face of temptation, and how it preys upon our own lusts and cravings, how can we overcome such a foe? Does the Bible provide any hope?

Joseph

In Samson we saw a man who dealt with temptation improperly, but in Joseph we have the perfect role model. Joseph is an interesting character because God blessed him despite some enormous trials and difficulties in his life. Though sold into Egyptian slavery by his own brothers, his faithfulness and God's sovereign plan elevated Joseph to a position of leadership in the house of Potiphar, an Egyptian ruler. Joseph had become a "top dog" and had everything a young Hebrew could dream of in the country of Egypt. But that did not rescue him from temptation. That's an important point to remember. You can have a good family, a car, plenty of money, and success in school, but none of those things will keep you from having to deal with temptation.

Joseph's temptation was a biggie. Potiphar's wife had her eye on him. She didn't bother with any small talk. She would come to him saying, "Joseph, come lie with me." She knew what she wanted, and she had a practice, no doubt, of getting her own way. Now Joseph was a young man with the same passion and curiosity that any young man his age would have. This was no routine temptation; the cards were stacked against him: He was young, no doubt she was beautiful, the house was empty, and her husband was gone. And the temptation came every single day; she wouldn't give up. It would have been so easy to fall; the risks seemed few.

But Joseph refused to yield, and he tells us why in his reply to Potiphar's wife. It wasn't that he feared she might get pregnant, or that Potiphar would find out. Those weren't his concerns. Joseph's response was, "How then can I do this great wickedness, and sin against God?" (Genesis 39:9). It was quite simple: Joseph loved the Lord and didn't want to displease Him. That is the only good reason to resist temptation. If we shun sin only because we fear the repercussions—though any deterrent is better than falling with temptation. The only lasting deterrent is loving God. If the penalty is the only thing that keeps us from sin, and the penalty is lifted, we will freely sin and turn our backs on God. Besides, we have plenty of evidence today that penalties are not a strong enough deterrent. If they were, we would see a drastic reduction of AIDS, herpes, and teenage pregnancies. We need to recognize what David realized following his sin against Bathsheba when he wrote: "Against You, You only, have I sinned" (Psalm 51:4). David knew he had sinned against *God*. If he had considered that truth at the time he first laid eyes on Bathsheba, he would not have fallen.

Joseph had to face an empty house and the enticements of a beautiful woman. Many young people today face similar circumstances. A study of four hundred 12- to 15-year-olds revealed that 40 percent of those living in single-parent families had participated in sexual relations at home after school.[4] It used to be that the problem of temptation was faced in the backseat of a car at the drive-in movies, but now it's at home when Mom and Dad are at work! Joseph faced the same dilemma. We can only imagine how enticing Potiphar's wife's alluring tactics were: "No one's at home; no one will find out; I won't tell anyone, Joseph; I will protect your reputation." What we do know is that this woman was persistent. In her frustration over his purity, she finally grabbed his clothing and pulled him down. At this point it seemed inevitable that he would fall, but Joseph used his only remaining alternative—he ran like crazy. He ran so fast that he left her holding his garment. He ran from the clutches of evil, from the grasp of sin and death, to the outstretched arms of the One that he loved most—his Lord and Savior.

This is a great example of the promise in 1 Corinthians 10:13: "God is faithful, who will not allow you to be tempted beyond what you are able, but with the temptation will also make the way of escape." Sometimes the only way to escape is to get up and run!

The temptation in Joseph's life, as in Samson's life, was initiated by Satan but allowed by God. You ask, "Why does God let me be tempted? Why doesn't He take temptation away?" Because temptation can have positive effects too! The greatest gift that God gave man was his ability to choose. If we really desire to follow the Lord, to choose Him over sin, then temptation will only drive us into His loving arms. Is there any better place to be? I have heard it said that Christians are like tea bags; you don't know what they're made of until you put them in hot water. Sometimes it's hot water that determines what I'm really made of. It's easy to *talk* the Christian faith, but a whole different thing to *walk* it. When the times of testing and temptation come, that's when we see what we're really made of!

It's important to know that God Himself is not unfamiliar with temptation. Jesus was also tempted, as Scripture says: He "was in all points tempted as we are, yet without sin" (Hebrews 4:15). Jesus did not really have the capacity to sin, because He was God, yet He was tempted. Why did He go through it? The Bible says that it was so we may know that we have someone in heaven who understands what we are going through. We cannot say of God, "He just sits on His throne, with no sin in His nature, while we're down here with all this garbage around us. He doesn't know the pressure we face." The fact is that Jesus came to this planet and walked it as a man, going through the same kind of garbage we go through. And He stands with us now, ready to get us through every temptation, if we'll only let Him.

Jesus handled temptation throughout His earthly life and in the face of the most difficult circumstances. He went toe-to-toe with Satan in the wilderness, rebuffing every temptation regarding food, possessions, and glory. He did it using the Word of God. He did it because He knew that His heavenly Father had provided for His every need. He did it because He knew His purpose in life and was obedient to it. And what was that purpose? Jesus had victory over every temptation for one reason: that He might go to the cross for us as a perfect and blameless sacrifice for sin. He knew that the only way for you and me to know God was for Him to go to that cross and die.

When Jesus hung on the cross He spoke three words that would forever change the power that sin can have in a person's life: *"It is finished."* What was finished? Satan's stranglehold on your life! You don't have to be under Satan's thumb any longer. In Colossians 2:15 we're told that Jesus "disarmed principalities and powers . . . triumphing over them."

If we're to experience victory over sin we must first recognize that by our own strength we cannot effectively resist temptation. Second, we must come to the cross of Jesus and admit that we have sinned and then receive His forgiveness (1 John 1:9). The third step, in response to the second, is to stay as close to Him as possible through prayer, study of His Word, and fellowship with other Christians. Finally, we need to keep a healthy distance from *anyone* or *anything* that might drag us down again into sin. When Satan comes knocking at my door I like to say to God, "Lord, would You mind getting that?"

Stand your ground in God's strength and you'll effectively deal with temptation!

God's Call
to the Young

9

God's Call to the Young

If, as a young person, you've made it to this point in the
book, you're probably wondering what "God's Call to the
Young" could possibly have to do with teenage suicide,
peer pressure, the temptation of sex and drugs, and other
topics we've discussed. The answer is simple: God calls
light out of darkness. He replaces sorrow with joy, tempo-
ral with eternal, death with life. God's Word is not simply a
list of "Do nots" but also a list of "Do's". You will find that
when God says what not to do in His Word, He also tells
you what to do! Second Timothy 2:22 tells us to "flee
youthful lusts," but then it goes on to say, "Pursue righteousness." I believe young people today are looking for
purpose, direction, a cause. Undoubtedly we find that
purpose laid out in God's Word. It entails being fully committed to Jesus Christ and having the willingness and
availability to live for Him each day of our lives.

In Acts 2:17 we're told that in the last days God will pour
out His Spirit on all flesh, and His sons and daughters will
prophesy. I believe one of the signs of the last days is that
God will be using young people. We've seen evidence of
this already, especially in the "Jesus Movement" of the
seventies. I believe that it is God's desire to continue moving upon the hearts of today's young people and to use them
in a mighty way. It's been my experience that young people
are generally not as "hung up" as people who have gotten a
little bit older and more set in their ways. They're often

more open and more pliable. These characteristics are part of being a servant of the Lord.

When I survey the landscape of today's teenagers I can't help but think of a young person in Scripture by the name of Jeremiah, who came face-to-face with God's calling in his life. God used this young man to speak to His people. That was his calling. However, before Jeremiah could be used by God he first had to make a decision, a decision to live God's way and to stand up for what was right regardless of what other people wanted him to do. In like fashion God is looking for young people today who will step forward and say, "Here I am, Lord, send me. I'm ready to go. I'm ready to serve. I'm ready to do what You want me to do."

In Ephesians 2:2 we read, "You once walked according to the course of this world, according to the prince of the power of the air, the spirit who now works in the sons of disobedience." The phrase "You once walked" actually implies "to browse or wander about loosely with no aim or purpose." Before coming to know Christ we were all without purpose; we were just wandering about with no real direction. Another phrase in this passage, "according to the course," conveys the idea of a weather vane. This gives us a clear picture of what is being said. Before a person becomes a Christian he is like a weather vane going whichever way the wind is blowing. But when a person commits his life to Christ he should no longer be driven to and fro by the winds of the world. Having repented, the new spiritual nature has an intense desire to follow God and do His will. God is looking for that kind of disciple today, the person whom He can direct.

Jesus challenged a great multitude of people who were following Him to just such discipleship. He asked them to pick up the cross and follow Him. That is what God desires of today's youth as well (and for all Christians)—that they take up the cross and follow Jesus Christ. It means dying to the old nature and committing to walk in newness of life. It means finding God's will and purpose and making it top priority. To many people this is somewhat frightening, but I have discovered that God's plan for me is far better than any plans I could make for myself.

The prevailing mood in society today is that to be successful one must be self-reliant, independent, "your own man." One study done among college-age youth revealed the type of life that most would try to forge for themselves. The article was titled "Freshmen Want Cash, Not Ideals" and said in part, "Today's college freshmen are more interested in making big money and less interested in pondering the meaning of life than students twenty years ago, a study of almost six million freshmen reveals. . . . Seventy percent of freshman in 1985 rated being well off financially as important, up from 43% in 1966. . . . Freshmen seem to have embraced the idea of making a lot of money as a kind of philosophy of life itself."[1] Consequently, the goals for many young people today are materially influenced—getting a Porsche, living in a nice house, having a lot of money, or going on expensive vacations. This type of philosophy is setting a dangerous precedent for today's Christian teenagers. Few are making a decision to really follow Christ and to live a life of denial and sacrifice.

Our daily newspapers print all the warnings necessary to avoid the meaningless material pursuits of many people in the "baby boom" generation. One article put it this way: "Many of the most successful baby boomers are finding their jobs are long on salary but short on satisfaction, a situation some psychologists say can lead to serious emotional problems."[2] The article pointed out that the "boomers" and the more affluent "yuppies" are shaping the direction of our culture and in the process are finding mountains of stress. To deal with the weight of success, the "boomers" are said to have embraced everything from aerobics to Zen, but "many find they still have the feeling that something is missing." One 39-year-old lawyer who worked enormously long hours in a very boring and meaningless activity was cited as a good example of the problems of this generation. Though she earned a tremendous amount of money, she ended up at the desk of her boss begging for "meaningful" work.

Young people today need to realize that the generation preceding them has equated materialism with success and come away with an empty heart. We must recognize that the most important thing in life is not making a lot of bucks but doing God's will. That's the life of commitment Jesus is looking for today.

Jeremiah

Jeremiah lived in a time very similar morally to the time we are living in right now. In fact the backdrop of society that he was called to was very dark. The people had turned their backs on God. They were involved in idol worship, sexual impurity was out of control, violent crimes were prevalent, and people were offering their children as sacrifices to the idols they worshiped. I don't think things have changed very much. I find that in our culture, with all its enlightenment and technology and so-called sophistication, we still face the same moral problems. In many ways our society is without absolutes and without morals. We even find people who are offering their children to idols. I don't mean child sacrifice in the way it was practiced in Jeremiah's time; we do it differently today. We call it abortion. Each year 1.5 million children are killed before birth, and most of those victims are the result of sexual permissiveness. Abortion has become a form of birth control. In Jeremiah's day they had their pagan gods; today people are offering their unborn children on the altar of abortion to another pagan god—the god of lust. Though we call him modern, man hasn't really changed.

In this context let's read the words of Jeremiah:

> The word of the Lord came to me, saying "Before I formed you in the womb I knew you; before you were born I sanctified you; and I ordained you a prophet to the nations." Then I said, "Ah, Lord God! Behold, I cannot speak, for I am a youth." But the Lord said to me, "Do not say, 'I am a youth,' for you shall go to all to whom I shall send you, and whatever I command you, you shall speak. Do not be afraid of their faces, for I am with you to deliver you," says the Lord. Then the Lord put forth His hand and touched my mouth, and the Lord said to me, "Behold, I have put My words in your mouth. See, I have this day set you over the nations and over the kingdoms, to root out and to pull down, to destroy and to throw down, to build and to plant" (Jeremiah 1:4-10).

Jeremiah further describes the condition of the people in the sixth chapter of his book saying, "From the least to the greatest, everyone is given over to covetousness." It's interesting that of all the words he could have used to summarize the mentality of the time, he uses this word "covetousness," which means "the greedy desire to have more, no matter what it costs you or somebody else." He goes on to say that from the least to the greatest, everyone was given over to covetousness, and they were not ashamed when they did these things, and couldn't even blush. Isn't that typical of the time in which we are living? No shame, no remorse, no sadness over the sins that have been committed by so many.

That generation was ripe for judgment, and I think the parallel to our society is evident—we too are ripe for judgment. But God, the Scripture says, has no delight in the death of the wicked. He doesn't want to judge us. We are assured that "He is longsuffering toward us, not willing that any should perish but that all should come to repentance" (2 Peter 3:9). But enough is enough. There is coming a time when God's judgment is going to fall. In the meantime, He is looking for people to come to Him, and He is looking for people that He can call His representatives.

He searches today for young people like Jeremiah who at the time of his calling was probably around 17 years of age. He was a pliable, flexible, open young man, willing to do whatever God wanted him to do. Surely there were many people whom God could have called. He could have called a great warrior, a brave and fearless man. But instead he chose an insecure, timid, maybe even acne-faced teenager. Jeremiah was a young man who was not very confident, as is seen by his reply to God's call on his life: "I cannot speak, for I am a youth." He did not perceive himself as God's gift to humanity. I have found that God is looking for people who are not full of themselves. Instead He looks for persons, like a Jeremiah, who are wholly reliant on God's ability because they have recognized their own inability. It's a principle we find throughout Scripture, as in 1 Corinthians 1:27: "God has chosen the foolish things of the world to put to shame the wise, and God has chosen the weak things of the world to put to shame the things which are mighty."

David

Another man who illustrates this principle is David. He, like Jeremiah, was a teenager when God called him to be the king over Israel. God had spoken to the prophet Samuel and told him to anoint a new king because He had rejected the current king, Saul, for his disobedience. He told Samuel to go to the house of Jesse in Bethlehem, where He would show him the man he wanted. So Samuel came to Jesse's house and proclaimed, "I'm here to anoint a king." That, of course, appealed to Jesse, so he called his sons out to be examined by the prophet. But Jesse overlooked David, leaving him to tend the sheep. As his sons stood in a line we can imagine the pride Jesse must have felt—one of his strapping young sons A KING! But as Samuel walked up the line looking at each of the brothers, the Lord kept telling him, "This is not the one."

Having failed to find the right man, Samuel asked Jesse, "Do you have any other sons?" To this Jesse gave a reply that revealed exactly what he thought of his young son, David: "There remains yet the youngest, and there he is, keeping the sheep." It is interesting, and a little sad, that the word used here for youngest does not apply only in terms of years. It actually implies that he was the "least esteemed" of all of Jesse's sons. Jesse was embarrassed to admit he was there. But as David came in, God told Samuel that he was the man, so Samuel anointed David to be the king over all of Israel.

Can you imagine the envy of David's brothers? Their little kid brother was chosen over them! It's a wonderful display of God's sovereign choosing, and an example of the timber he looks for in men. People that you or I would think should be a mighty instrument in God's plan are often the very ones God cannot use because they, like everyone else, look at the outward appearance. As a result they tend to trust too much in their own abilities and not enough in God's.

It wasn't until later, when David battled with the giant, Goliath, that people saw in him what God had known all along. But even as he came to the battle lines, where the nine-foot-six Philistine stood taunting the fearful soldiers of Israel, David's brother, Eliab, treated him as a nobody. He told David to go back home to his sheep. David was rejected in his own home, by his father and brothers. He knew what it was like to not receive the love and attention that he wanted. As we've seen, this is a common experience today for many kids who come from homes where they simply don't get any attention—perhaps because the parents are too busy or are divorced. Far too many of today's teenagers feel that their parents simply don't care.

Both David and Jeremiah knew what it was like to be called into God's service at a young age. But neither of them backed away from what God wanted him to do. David and Jeremiah stood in the power of God's might, and not in their own. We can have the same confidence to know that we'll never stand out there alone. This is what gave strength to the three Hebrew young men that we looked at earlier. Though they were thrown headlong into the fiery furnace, a fourth person walked with them. It was none other than Jesus Christ. We can know that Jesus walks with us in like manner. If you are a young person serving God today, there will be the fiery furnaces of evolution being taught as fact at school, backbiting friends, self-consciousness, parents who may not understand your desire to please God, and on and on. But knowing and believing that Jesus is there to walk every valley with you is an important aspect of being used by God.

There was a man in church history whose name was Sebastian, an officer of the Imperial Guard of Rome and also a follower of Jesus Christ. He would not renounce his faith in Christ and acknowledge that Caesar was Lord. For this he was shot by the firing squad of the day—with bows and arrows. When his Christian friends came to retrieve his body, they found that miraculously Sebastian had survived. So they nursed him back to health. As soon as Sebastian was able he was back preaching to the very people who had tried to kill him. This so infuriated the people that they tried again, and this time they succeeded. How could a person do something like that? I believe he had the hope and full assurance that God was with him.

God told Jeremiah, "Whatever I command you, you shall speak." I like the literal translation of that verse, because what it really says is this: "Whatever errand I send you on, you shall go." That's really all we are—God's errand boys or errand girls. God has sent us on an errand for Him, and has given each of us certain things to do. When I was about 18 I used to go down to my church, Calvary Chapel of Costa Mesa, looking for an opportunity to do something for God. One day I went to the pastor, Chuck Smith, and said, "Chuck, I believe that God has called me to serve Him, and I would like to do something for God." So Pastor Chuck sent me to see one of his associate pastors. When I talked to him and told him of my desire, instead of giving me a Bible and an office, he handed me a broom. He told me to sweep up the leaves of a pepper tree nearby.

Now this tree was always dropping leaves, so day after day I swept the dumb leaves of this tree. I started thinking, "Now isn't this wonderful! Here I am wanting to serve God, and I'm sweeping under a tree." I can remember that when all the pastors would go to lunch, I would go into the church office and just sit there, hoping that someone might use me in some capacity. I can remember hearing the secretary answer the phone: "Hello, Calvary Chapel. . . . Do you need a counselor or minister, someone to pray for you or talk with you?" She would look around through all the offices, as if I were invisible, then pick up the phone and say, "Sorry, there's no one here. Please call back in 45 minutes."

Finally my day came. I was summoned by Pastor Chuck, who said, "Greg, we have a job for you to do."

I replied, "Yes I'm ready! What is it? Go to Uganda, preach the gospel? Anything—you tell me!"

"We want you to buy a doorknob for the church office."

Wow, a doorknob! I was excited. I got the money and I walked into the department store as if I were on a holy mission of God. I was so happy to be chosen to acquire a doorknob for the Lord. When I found the doorknob section, I was faced with more doorknobs than I'd ever seen before in my whole life. There seemed to be hundreds of them. I checked them all out, from standard to deluxe. Finally I picked out the one I thought would work, then went back and proudly presented it to Pastor Chuck. It was the wrong size! But I wasn't discouraged. I believed that God had given me something to do, and I wanted to do it to the best of my ability.

The point is that if you want to be a person whom God can use, you have to do what He sets before you *today*. It's not wrong to want to do something of great service for the Lord, but it's just that He would rather have you do what He wants in the meantime. I believe that God sends many little tests into our lives to see if we will be faithful in the small things. When the time comes, and God prompts you to share his love with somebody, do you respond by saying, "I haven't got time; I have more important things to do"? That's failing His test. He may bring you back to it again and again, and though it seems small, it's just one of His many ways of molding and shaping us. I believe, even to this day, that God puts things in my path to see if I'll be faithful.

He'll ask the same of you. Let's not forget that David was on a simple little errand for his father when he ended up defeating Goliath. When David woke up that morning I don't think he said, "Let's see, what can I do today? Maybe I'll go to the valley of Elah and kill this giant guy named Goliath, and then everyone will know I'm a big hero!" He didn't think of that. He probably got up thinking, "Today I'll tend my little flock of sheep, like I do every day." But his father called him in and asked him to take food to his brothers on the front line of battle against the Philistines. David didn't reply, "Father, that's too menial for me. Don't you remember that the prophet came and anointed me to be king? That's too insignificant; I'm too important." No, David grabbed the food and was out the door. And because he was faithful, God had a far greater test for him in the valley of Elah, which, as we all know, he passed with flying colors.

I wonder, are you passing your tests right now? Perhaps one day you'd like to be a missionary, or a preacher, or an evangelist who would reach thousands for Christ. Then why not start with your next-door neighbors? Have you told them about Jesus Christ? How about some of the kids who sit next to you in school? How about people you run into every day—when's the last time you told one of them about the Lord? You see, you've got to start with what is in front of you right now. On whatever errand God sends you, that is what you should do.

God has an errand for us all. What is it? It's found in Matthew 28: "Preach the gospel to every person." Are you following that commission? God has called every one of us to share our faith. When was the last time you told someone about Jesus Christ? When was the last time you asked someone if he would like to commit his life to Christ? When was the last time you obeyed the marching orders that Jesus has given you as a part of His church?

Some people believe they're not called to share the gospel with others because they're not knowledgeable enough or because they're too shy. The first time I prayed with a person to receive Christ, I had only been a Christian for about two weeks. I didn't know anything about the Bible and I had never told anyone about Jesus, but I really wanted to. As I was walking along the beach I saw this middle-aged lady sitting on a towel and I thought, "I'll go to her and share what Christ has done for me." So I sat down next to her and said, "Can I tell you a little bit about God? I have this little booklet I want to read to you." She replied, "Sure, go ahead."

The booklet I had was called "The Four Spiritual Laws," and I knew so little that I hadn't even memorized it yet. I actually read it to her, starting with page 1: "Just as there are physical laws that govern the physical universe, so are there spiritual laws that govern your relationship with God. Law One: God loves you and has a wonderful plan for your life. . . ." On I went, straight through the booklet. It ended with this question: "Is there any reason you shouldn't accept Christ right now?"

I looked up at her as I asked it, and she said, "No."

I was startled. "No?"

"No," she said again.

"Does that mean yes, you *want* to accept Christ?" I asked. And she replied, "Yes."

At that point I panicked. "What do I do now?" I thought. In an attempt to buy time I asked her to bow her head for prayer, trying to sound as reverent as possible. As she did, I frantically ripped through that little book, hoping that there would be a prayer in there somewhere. Finally I found it! I prayed with her, and after we were done she looked up and something had happened to her. I could actually see that Christ had come into her life! Because I took a little bit of time out of my day, I had the privilege of being used by God to help a person pass from darkness to light, from hell to heaven. One person's eternal destiny literally changed because I was willing to take the opportunity presented by the Lord.

Don't get me wrong—God doesn't want to use us because He needs us. God wants to use us because He loves us. He desires for us to participate in His plans and in His purposes and on His errands. That's what God said to Jeremiah, and the same is true in principle for us. We have an errand to run; let's get started on it. Let's tell people about what God can do. Jeremiah 1:5 says, "Before I formed you in the womb I knew you; before you were born I sanctified you; and I ordained you a prophet to the nations." God knew long before Jeremiah was even conceived that he would be His man. David echoes this same thought in Psalm 139:13,15: "You have formed my inward parts; You have covered me in my mother's womb. . . . My frame was not hidden from You when I was made in secret."

In the womb, David said, God called me, God ordained me, God had a plan for my life. God knows those who will commit their lives to Him. I thank God for that, because I can look back on the past that I had as a kid and on all the difficulties that I had in coming from a broken home and know that somehow God has been able to use it all. I'm not glad I went through all the hardship, but I'm glad that God could turn it around and use it for His glory. He knew that at the ripe old age of 17, when I was walking across my high-school campus, I was going to hear His gospel and respond to it. He knew that a couple of years later He was going to call me to preach the gospel. He knew that I would be doing what I am doing today. And He knows what I am going to be doing later. He is the Alpha and the Omega, the first and the last. He was present when my life began, and He'll be there when He takes me home. He called me, and He has a call in your life as well, because we have all been called to serve Him in some capacity.

How about you? Are you running God's errands right now? Are you ready to step forward and say, "Here I am Lord, send me"?

Scripture tells us, "The eyes of the Lord run to and fro throughout the whole earth, to show Himself strong on behalf of those whose heart is loyal to Him" (2 Chronicles 16:9). I love that! God isn't looking for strong people; He's looking for people He can be strong on behalf of. He's looking for someone who will say, "Lord, I don't have a lot of ability, but I do have *availability*. Here I am; send me." Would you be such a person? God can use you as a young person. The apostle Paul told Timothy, "Let no one despise your youth, but be an example to the believers in word, in conduct, in love, in spirit, in faith, in purity" (1 Timothy 4:12). Don't look at your age as a liability; look at it as an asset. God can use everybody, young or old, if they'll just volunteer.

Are you available? I hope so. We're not here by accident. We're not here just to chart our own destiny, or to do what we think is right. If you will commit yourself to the God who created you, and purpose in your heart to follow His plan no matter what your circumstances, and keep yourself available to His call, I can guarantee that you'll never sink to the point of despair that would cause you to want to take your own life.

Family in Crisis

10

Family in Crisis

I believe that the breakdown in the family is a major reason why our country is in such miserable shape today. *A family may be able to exist without a country, but a country cannot exist without the family!* I picture the family/country relationship as something like that of a hub to a wheel. The spokes that come out of the hub (the family) represent the many issues and problems facing our nation today. But clearly the breakdown of the wheel (our country) is in the center, in the hub. This is what is impairing the whole wheel's performance. I believe that the rise of drug abuse, teenage pregnancy, violent crime, homosexuality, and teen suicide are spokes within the wheel, and they all come back to the hub, the broken home. C. S. Lewis once said, "The home must be the foundation of our national life. . . . When all is said and done, it is in the home that the character is formed, it is there that we appear as we really are."

Within the social framework of the American family we find that one of the primary elements in dealing with adolescent suicide is that of the parent-teen relationship. It would be unfair and horribly cruel to make the parents of suicide victims scapegoats who are solely responsible for this epidemic. On the other hand, it would be a serious oversight to ignore the importance of the parental role in the life of today's teens. If there was ever a time when teenagers needed their parents' confidence, their parents' support, their parents' discipline, their parents' love, that time is today. Yet many of today's parents were themselves victims of the sixties "me" generation. As everyone knows, it was a generation of young people who were oriented toward self-fulfillment and self-gratification. As a result, many of these parents suffer from a real lack of concern about their children. A lot of hippies have turned into yuppies and have exchanged their VW's for BMW's. They've exchanged their frayed blue jeans and sandals for designer clothing and have flip-flopped in material values from the "have-nots" to the "have-a-lots." Material things, which were once protested against, are now contested for. Materialism in the eighties has become a point of focus and a new god for many people.

In essence, what is happening to our preteens and teens today is that they are being *left to themselves*. We have let other people take the responsibility for our children. We haven't given them what they need in the home, and now we are beginning to reap what we have sown. Proverbs 29:15 presents this type of parenting with an ominous warning, "A child left to himself brings shame to his mother." Why is a child left to go his own direction a grief to his mother? Because, the Scripture says, "Foolishness is bound in a heart of the child." Children, like you and I, are simply sinners, and with only a sinful nature to guide them, they'll naturally go the wrong way, especially if they're left to themselves.

An article about morality in *U.S. News & World Report* stated: " 'Teaching values has always been a cooperative effort by the family and the social institutions,' " says Clark University philosopher Christina Hoff Sommers. " 'Parents could count on honesty being taught in the church or the synagogue, or in the Boy Scouts, but now you have television instead, but it's hard to see what moral values, if any, are taught by TV.' "[1] It should also be noted that by the time a typical student graduates from high school, he or she has spent more hours with television (15,000 hours) than with teachers (12,000 hours).[2] *USA Today* reported, "The TV has replaced the fireplace" as the primary place for family gatherings.

I would not say that television is merely *amoral*; I would say that it's *immoral* to a large degree. God does not exist in "television land," for the most part. God does not exist in sitcoms. God does not exist in the soap operas. Seldom, if ever, are we shown on TV a person turning to God in prayer. Rarely, if ever, do we see a Christian portrayed accurately. For the most part a Christian is portrayed on TV as some wild-eyed fanatic or brainwashed bigot. (Perhaps there have been some realistic portrayals, but I have not seen any.) To sum it up, this is what our children are learning in TV land: There is no God, and life really works out quite well because in the last six minutes of any given program all of life's difficulties are resolved.

Yes, life always works out in time for a commercial break. I believe this 15,000 hours in front of TV is having a dramatic effect on the minds of today's children. Have you sat down recently and watched what they are serving to children on Saturday morning? It's frightening, and yet so many children are being left to themselves. Is it any wonder that we have a generation of juvenile delinquents?

If that statement sounds harsh, consider this statement issued by the police department of Houston, Texas. In this sarcastic appeal to their community they tell a person "How to raise a juvenile delinquent in eight easy steps."

1. Begin to give the child everything he wants at infancy, and he will grow up to believe the world owes him a living.
2. When he picks up bad words, laugh about it. This will make him think he is cute. It will also encourage him to pick up cuter phrases that will blow off the top of your head later.
3. Never give him any spiritual training. Wait until he is 21, then let him decide for himself.

4. Avoid the use of the word "wrong"; it might help him develop a guilt complex. This will condition him to believe later, when he is arrested for stealing a car, that society is against him and he is being persecuted.
5. Pick up everything he leaves lying around: books, shoes, clothes, etc. Do everything for him so he will be experienced in throwing all responsibility on others.
6. Let him read any material he can get his hands on, or watch any program he wants to watch. Be careful that the glasses he drinks out of are sterilized, but let his mind feast on garbage.
7. Quarrel frequently in the presence of your children. In this way they will not be too shocked when the home is broken up later.
8. Give a child all the spending money he wants. Never let him earn his own. Why should he have things as tough as you had them?[3]

Children are being left to themselves. If that is not bad enough, many of today's parents are behaving no better than children themselves. They haven't grown up. They haven't grown out of that selfish, "me-first" attitude that came as a result of the "me generation's" craving for self-satisfaction. This type of philosophy continues to be the dominant trait of many in the "baby boom" generation. One result is the increase of two-career families—an increase that is based not on need but on a desire to live in nicer homes, drive nicer cars, and take nicer vacations. Of course, it also means less time spent with the children. Many marriages end today with the muttering of these commonly heard phrases "We just aren't happy anymore," "I wasn't finding fulfillment any longer," and "We had irreconcilable differences." Some might venture to ask, "But what about the children?" only to hear the reply,

"They'll be all right. Children are resilient; they always bounce back."

Fathers, it seems, have grown increasingly weak as role models in our country. One study showed that the average father spends less than 30 seconds a day with his child![4] That's further proof of the need for Christian men to assume their biblical roles within the family structure and become the first line of defense to help stem the problem of breakups in marriage and breakdowns in the family. In fact, noted Christian family counselor James Dobson feels that the Western world now stands at a great crossroads in its history, and that its survival as a people depends on the presence or absence of masculine leadership in the home.

It's unfortunate, but many times, because of the frantic pace of our society, parents simply don't take time to listen to their kids. It's somewhat ironic that when our children are young we encourage them to speak their first words, but once they start talking it seems we spend the rest of their childhood telling them "BE QUIET!"

This is a parental habit pattern that can be very harmful to children. And these patterns can start with seemingly innocent little incidents. You're approached by your child after church when he has just completed his first rendition of God—scribbled marks of purple crayon on a piece of paper. That is important! If you don't take time to look at that little drawing because you're in a rush, that's the beginning of a pattern of not communicating, of not paying attention. After years of this, a child learns that the only time he can get your wholehearted attention is when he does something wrong. In essence, you're saying to your child, "If you want my attention, do something bad."

Similarly, I believe one of the main things that drives young people away from Jesus Christ is hypocrisy in the mother or father who claims to follow Jesus. Obviously we all fall short; every one of us slips up at home. In fact, it may be the setting where we slip up most often. But we need to go to our child when we've done wrong and say, "I'm wrong. I'm sorry I raised my voice. Daddy was under a lot of pressure, and I apologize." Such a simple, honest confession can make a significant difference in our child's eyes. Yet often we refuse to admit we are wrong. We steadfastly cling to the false assumption that an authority figure shouldn't admit to weakness or fault. It's easier to protect our pride by squelching an argument with the words "SHUT UP!" or "GO TO YOUR ROOM!" Such is the pattern for developing a rebellious child right under your nose.

Those patterns of poor communication developed when the child is young later grow into harsh demands such as "GET IN THE CAR—IT'S TIME TO GO TO CHURCH AND WORSHIP GOD." If you succeed in getting your child into the car, you're apt to pull into the parking lot with the windows rolled up and yourself screaming something like "SIT BACK AND SHUT UP! YOU'RE GOING WHETHER YOU LIKE IT OR NOT!" This phenomenon is common to many Christians, I'm sure. The hypocrisy comes in when you see these same people open their car doors and emerge with smiling faces and choruses of "Praise the Lord! How are you, brother?"

Can you see what this teaches an impressionable child? I can almost see the gears turning in his mind, saying, "So that's what it is; when you go to church you're acting. It's like when I pretend to play army; I'm pretending to be something I'm really not. So when I go to church I know God, but when I go home I behave quite differently." If this is what we teach our children, why should we be shocked when they rebel as teenagers or withdraw from us?

Another bent spoke on our country's wheel is the crime rate. Children who are neglected affect the crime rate tremendously, especially violent crime. A documentary by ABC called "The Crime in America Report" said that teenagers account for one-third of all violent-crime arrests in Los Angeles. And the number one criminal in our nation is between the ages of 15 and 20. In 1981, 18-year-olds committed more robberies than criminals of any other age, and 19-year-olds committed more murders.[5] This dilemma has prompted one person to accurately conclude, "The cure for crime is not in the electric chair, but in the high chair." In other words, start them young and teach them what is right.

An article I read in *Pulpit Helps* bears this out. It began with the headline "A Child Brought Up in Bible School Is Seldom Brought Up in Court" and went on to report:

> Lee Baxton was a businessman who served as a city mayor for two years. During this time he presided over mayor's court, hearing some 2400 cases. He made a standing offer to pay the court costs of any person convicted of a criminal offense if that person had been regular in Sunday school attendance during that year. There were many who said they used to attend "a long time ago" or "I plan to go when I am released," but not once in 2400 cases did he ever have to pay anyone's fine.[6]

I don't believe this means that Sunday school is a cure-all. But I certainly believe that it reduces the chance for problems down the road if a spiritual foundation is being laid in the child's life. The breakdown of family and moral values is an important reason why youth crime is escalating. Variables such as family stability and the degree of parental affection and discipline which a child receives make a significant difference.

So here we have the problem. The hub of the wheel is cracked, and the spokes are bent or broken. We've seen various campaigns to help fight the battles of drug abuse, teen pregnancies, and suicide. These programs are trying to straighten out the spokes of the wheel, and I commend any effort, for example, to stop the abuse of drugs. However, one recent study found that such programs have very little effect in stopping children from taking drugs.[7] Kids are not concerned about scare tactics. When these programs come across with a message such as "Don't take drugs or you will die," they often make such temptations even more daring and exciting. This same report went on to say that real change only occurs when on the inside, out of personal volition, each person chooses to change because of moral beliefs. Yet this is not being addressed by the many well-meaning campaigns.

However, we as Christians can address it, and it begins by laying a biblical foundation in the home. It comes back to heeding what God has to say. If ever there was a need in our country for a spiritual revival, that time is now. Because we have legislated God out of our classroom, and because we have legislated Him out of so many other facets of our national life, we now reap the results. The situation is desperate. And the solution starts with us. As Christians we must examine our homes, asking the questions "Am I really the Christian parent I should be? Am I really a godly father and leader? Am I really a godly mother?" In our final chapter we will examine in more detail some of the things that Scripture says about marriage and parenting.

Help for Parents

11

Help for Parents

Dealing with the loss of a child to suicide is one of the most painful of all human tragedies. Coping with the memories, the deep sense of loss, and the feelings of helplessness, anger, and unrelenting guilt can be overwhelming. If anybody ever wanted to walk back in time, it would be such a parent. But only Jesus can wipe away the past. When we came to Him initially, He held out His nail-pierced hands to us and made us this offer: "Old things have passed away; behold, all things have become new" (2 Corinthians 5:17). We know the apostle Paul was a forward-looking man. Though there were tragedies in his past that pulled at his heart and beckoned him to turn back, he said, "Forgetting those things which are behind . . . I press toward the goal for the prize of the upward call of God in Christ Jesus" (Philippians 3:13,14).

Grief must have its place, but grief will not change the past. If you're a parent who has lost a loved child to suicide, I urge you—don't look back! Surely you can carry the memories with you, those that are light and easy to bear, but unload those that burden, those that bring heartache. Unload the guilt, the fear, and the chains of the past onto the back of Him who is able to bear all our griefs and sins.

Deep-seated guilt often resides in the heart of a mom or a dad as a form of self-induced punishment. It's a way of kicking yourself for what happened, of bearing the responsibility. Surely you could have been a better parent in preventing the death of your child; it's true, and for that fact some of the guilt is founded. Yet even the best of parents have children that go astray. Might I remind you that our heavenly Father, the only perfect parent, could only watch in sorrow as His children, Adam and Eve, chose the schemes of the devil over God's plan. Founded or unfounded, guilt will produce sorrow. That was God's intention, for godly sorrow brings repentance. But once repentance has come forth and forgiveness has been offered, guilt no longer has a purpose. If you're a parent facing guilt today, the question of responsibility is hard to face. But if you have faced it once, and if you have found that you were guilty, then take your guilt to Calvary and never pick it up again. It serves no further purpose. Jesus said that it was God's plan to turn our sorrows into joy. It starts by giving those sorrows to Him.

Fortunately, most parents will never have to deal with the tragedy of suicide. Yet every parent must deal with the fear of it, especially in today's social climate. So how does a parent prevent such a tragedy, if indeed, that is possible? Once again we must turn to God's Word, for in it we have been given all the instructions for righteous living.

We have seen how the American family faces a monumental crisis. Our culture has made the traditional family—father as breadwinner and mother as homemaker—nearly obsolete. In fact, only 7 percent of America's families live like this, while 93 percent of the families today are a combination of many variations. These would include stepfathers, stepmothers, single parents, and mixed families of divorce. A whopping 26.3 percent of families in America today have only one parent. As a result, we are facing difficulties that were unheard of 50 years ago.

Along with the change in family makeup has also come a change in family responsibilities. At the present time nearly 60 percent of all American households have a mother and father that both work full-time. This has resulted in a lot of confusion about the roles of husbands and wives. As I look at this situation, it seems that the emphasis is solely on personal happiness. Dr. Frederick Green of the Children's Hospital in Washington, D.C. has observed that children are becoming more expendable and are now seen as a burden to families. Parents are caught in a crunch of conflicting values, for they value children but they also value other things, such as time for themselves, material things, status, and their careers. So the children are treated as excess baggage.

Obviously, this impacts children in a negative way. In many homes today no father is present. One-third of all couples that were married in the seventies have divorced, leaving millions of children with only one parent in the home. Over a million children run away every year, most of them from middle-class families. Consider the types of problems that schoolteachers face today in contrast to those of a generation ago. Schoolteachers were asked in 1940 to describe the top several disciplinary problems they faced in the classroom. Those problems were:

- Talking
- Chewing gum
- Making noise
- Running in the halls
- Wearing improper clothing
- Not putting wastepaper in the wastebasket.

In the 1980's, educators were asked the same question by college researchers. Here are the top seven disciplinary problems that modern-day teachers must face:

- Rape
- Robbery
- Assault
- Burglary

rson
Bombing
Murder[2]

If there was ever a time to return to biblical standards for parenting, that time is now. Before we face the guilt that comes when our children become runaways, drug addicts, criminals, or suicide victims, we need to find the preventive measures laid out in God's Word. Proverbs 22:6 tells us, "Train up a child in the way he should go, and when he is old he will not depart from it." Some parents get very discouraged because this promise doesn't seem to work. They cart their children off to church every Sunday morning. They enroll them in Christian schools. They allow them to listen only to Christian music. They find them Christian playmates. They teach them to memorize Scripture. They send them to Christian summer camps. Yet when these children reach the age of adolescence they go into full rebellion. The parents walk away saying, "But we have been training up our child in the way he should go. What went wrong?" The question I must ask is this: Have we really been doing what is contained in this Scripture? Or have we only followed it to the letter of the law, while avoiding the spirit behind it?

I know it's very difficult to rear a teenager these days. Adolescence is a period of rapid changes. Yet through all the heartache, difficult decisions, changes, and differences that teens are experiencing at this time in their lives, as parents we should be the one stable thing in their lives.

So what does it mean to "train up a child in the way he should go"? Literally translated, it speaks of the actions of a Hebrew midwife who, after delivering a child, would dip her finger in crushed dates and put it into the baby's mouth, thus developing a thirst in the baby for milk. It also speaks of breaking and bringing into submission a wild horse by placing a rope in its mouth. So when we train up a child, our desire as parents should be to create a thirst in that child for God. Second, it means that we are to mold him and shape him, to put boundaries in his life—rights and wrongs, do's and don'ts. We're charged to break him of rebellion but not break him in spirit.

In one passage of Scripture this same Hebrew word for "child" refers to an infant. In another it refers to a young boy. In another passage it's used of Ishmael in his preteen years. It's also used to describe Joseph when he was 17. In another passage it describes a young man who is ready for marriage. Therefore, when we are told to train up a child—to create a thirst in him, and to bring him into submission—it is speaking of the years from infancy to young adulthood. We might retranslate this verse, "Create a thirst for God in your child. Build in him, from infancy to adulthood, the experience of submission."

It's been said that you can lead a horse to water but you can't make him drink. In like manner, we can't make our children love God. But I'll tell you one thing: Though you can't make a horse drink, you can sure salt his oats! Long ago the people who made popcorn in the movie theaters learned this great secret. They would sell the popcorn at bargain-basement prices, but when you began to eat it, it was so salty that you just had to get something to drink. That's when you found that the drinks were two dollars apiece! I have to admit, they did a good job of creating a thirst in me. That's precisely what we as parents are to do—create a thirst in our children to know God in a real and personal way. Your lifestyle, your example will be salt to your children.

The next phrase that must be examined in detail is "the way he should go." This does not mean that we train a child the way we as parents *personally* want him or her to go. Rather, it implies that through careful observation we search for our child's abilities and talents and appropriately direct him or her in them. Many parents want to live their lives through their children. Perhaps Dad wishes he had become a professional baseball player; maybe Mom wishes she had become a ballerina. Therefore their son or daughter ends up hopelessly trying to fulfill those frustrated dreams. I've seen this happen many times, and it's not what Scripture teaches us to do. In fact, Psalm 127:3 teaches us that children are a "heritage from the Lord," which means that they are a gift or a loan. It goes on to say that they are like arrows in a bow. And we are not the master of that bow. As parents we must submit our children as arrows to God; it is He who determines the direction the arrow will fly.

There is a wonderful illustration of this principle in Scripture where the Hebrew mothers kept bringing their children to Jesus. The original wording tells us that the mothers brought their children to dedicate them to Jesus. But the disciples, being hardened to the situation, rebuked these mothers and told them to go home, saying that the Master didn't have time for the kids. In their thinking, Jesus only had time for the multitudes. But Jesus rebuked the disciples and said, "Let the little children come to Me . . . for of such is the kingdom of heaven" (Matthew 19:14). With that He took them into His arms and blessed them. That's what we need to do. We need to bring our children and dedicate them to the Lord. It's a process of presenting our children over and over to Him, asking Him to help them and to help us as we raise them in the way they should go.

This phrase in the Hebrew, "the way he should go," also speaks of characteristics, manners, and modes in the lives of our children. Every child is different.

This, of course, can be seen in Scripture. We see rebellious children like Cain or like Absalom the son of David. On the other hand, David had another son named Solomon who was known for his wisdom. For a period in his life he was a godly person as well. So we see that each child has that bent or direction which he is naturally inclined to follow. Being aware of that, we want to observe those characteristics and manners and train each child accordingly. For example, we need to be sensitive to each child when it comes to discipline. For some children, discipline can be accomplished with only a word. For others, more tangible methods must be employed. We cannot treat each child the same in the area of discipline.

Finally, we need to examine the promise of this proverb: "When he is old he will not depart from it." The implication here is that when a child leaves home he will be spiritually equipped and mature. Putting the whole verse together, it should read this way: "Adapt the training of your child so it is in keeping with his God-given abilities and tendencies. When he comes to maturity, he will not depart from the thing he has received."

It's pretty much a certified conclusion that your children won't always appreciate the training and discipline they receive under your roof if it's done in a biblical manner, especially in their teenage years. But later they will thank you for it. It's funny how our perceptions of our parents change through the years. I came across a little clipping from a Dutch magazine that illustrates this point.

- At four years old the child says, "My daddy can do anything."
- At seven years he says, "My daddy knows a lot, a whole lot."
- At eight years, "My father doesn't quite know everything."
- At 12 years, "Oh, well, naturally my father doesn't know that either."
- At 14 years, "Father is hopelessly old-fashioned."
- At 21 years, "Oh, that man! He's out-of-date."
- At 25 years, "He knows a little bit about it, but not too much."

- At 30 years, "I must find out what Dad thinks about it."
- At 35 years, "Before we decide, we will go and get Dad's idea first."
- At 50 years, "What would Dad have thought about that?"
- At 60 years, "My dad knew literally everything."
- At 65 years, "I wish I could talk it over with Dad one more time."[3]

That may not soothe the wounds of a hurting parent who is facing a crisis with a rebellious teen, but it is true and it should give us a greater incentive to continue to "train up our children in the way they should go."

Now let's look at a familiar New Testament passage about parenting:

> Children, obey your parents in the Lord, for this is right. "Honor your father and mother," which is the first commandment with promise: "that it may be well with you and you may live long on the earth." And you, fathers, do not provoke your children to wrath, but bring them up in the training and admonition of the Lord (Ephesians 6:1-4).

The first verse in the passage—"Children, obey your parents in the Lord, for this is right"—is probably one of the most quoted by parents to children. But it should be understood that rebellious children are frequently the result of poor upbringing in the home. I think one primary reason our children don't choose to obey us is because we are inconsistent in our dealings with them. We tell them something is wrong, then slack off on it when we are not in the mood to enforce that guideline. We must stand by what we say as we lay out principles that are biblical and right.

As we rear our children we should have both positive initiative when they obey and negative consequences when they disobey. This is the biblical pattern of our heavenly Father. He told His people in Isaiah, "If you are willing and obedient, you shall eat the good of the land; but if you refuse and rebel, you shall be devoured." It's really quite simple. God says, "Do what I tell you to do and I will reward you. Disobey Me and you'll pay the price." The same should be true of our children. If they obey in the home, life will be great. If they disobey, consequences will follow. It must be understood that this includes discipline *and* reward. One of the greatest problems we have as parents is communicating to our children only when they do wrong. They simply don't get our attention when they've done well. We must reward them and let them know we are pleased when they clean their room, get a good grade on a paper, or complete their chores.

This promise in Ephesians is interesting in that it is quite severe: " 'Honor your father and mother,' which is the first commandment with promise: 'that it may be well with you and you may live long on the earth.' " In Old Testament times this was taken literally. If a son was rebellious or stubborn, if he refused to obey his parents, cursed them, and proved to be incorrigible, he was put to death. As you might guess, that eliminated most teenage rebellion! I'm not advocating such a system, since we're not under the Old Testament law anymore. But it certainly gets the point across.

Next, the apostle directs his attention to fathers by saying, "And you, fathers, do not provoke your children to wrath, but bring them up in the training and admonition of the Lord." In other words, it's our job as fathers to patiently instruct our children. In 1 Thessalonians 2:11,12 Paul reaffirms this practice when he writes, "You know how we exhorted, and comforted, and charged every one of you, as a father does his own children, that you would have a walk worthy of God." Once again there is that encouragement factor, building up our children and not just tearing down.

I think Moses gave us a great insight when he spoke to the Israelites about parenting: "Hear, O Israel. . . . You shall love the Lord your God with all your heart . . . soul, and . . . might. And these words which I command you today shall be in your heart; you shall teach them diligently to your children, and shall talk of them when you sit in your house, when you walk by the way, when you lie down, and when you rise up" (Deuteronomy 6:4-7). I like that. That's saying to teach our children all the time—not at just a given moment that we may call devotions, or during a special time of prayer, but *all* the time. When we sit down and when we rise up, Jesus should be a natural part of our home and conversation. When sitting at the dinner table, speak of the Lord. When taking a walk, speak of the Lord. Jesus can and should be brought into every facet of life, even in the TV programs you allow your children to watch. Jesus Christ desires to be a part of everything in your home. He needs to be thought of during playtime, during free time, and during work time. He must be present to help reinforce those absolutes that you've laid down. Your children may not like the current restraints that a holy God brings into your family right now, but they'll grow to love them, and Him, later on.

We're also instructed to discipline our children. Some parents have a problem with this. "I can't discipline my children," they protest. "I love them too much." I would take issue with that. In reality, if you do not discipline your children, I question your love. What kind of children are you raising? What are you teaching them? You're teaching them to do whatever they want, to have their own way. You're teaching them principles that aren't going to work very well in the real world. It is vital that we discipline our children so they learn that there is a right and there is a wrong. In Hebrews 12:5,6 God says, "My son, do not despise the chastening of the Lord, nor be discouraged when you are rebuked by Him; for whom the Lord loves He chastens." He says later in Hebrews that He disciplines us so that we might be partakers of His holiness. Applying that to us as parents, if we really love our children we will chasten them when necessary. The word "chasten" could also be translated "train as a son." It refers to God educating, nurturing, and disciplining His children. Therefore it includes not only the negative but also the positive side of nurturing our children.

Proverbs 13:24 tells us, "He who spares his rod hates his son, but he who loves him disciplines him promptly." We must establish boundaries in our homes. When you have little children, it's good to "child-proof" your home because little children love to explore. They will grab, throw, and play, and most of it is innocent. But we've all seen the young child who will walk up to the electric wall socket after being told not to (and sometimes after having been spanked) and defiantly hold his little finger as close to the forbidden fruit as possible. If ever there was a test of wills between parent and child, this is the time. It's a test of the boundaries that have been established, and it must be dealt with. It is a time of training.

The Bible says that foolishness is bound in the heart of a child. There's no doubt about it. It doesn't take long to discover that the same sin nature that is in you is in them as well. They test your authority. They test the boundaries you have set. For their own good you must back up what you say. Otherwise you are teaching them that whenever Mommy or Daddy says "no," eight warnings will follow. After the eighth warning Mommy will get so frustrated that something will happen. If this pattern continues, children will learn that once warned they have seven warnings left.

However, discipline often becomes nothing more than a way for a parent to vent frustration and anger. That's not the purpose of discipline. It's not license to blow your top. It must show your children that there is a right and a wrong, and that when the line is crossed they pay the price. That's life. That's what they will learn when they get out in the real world. That's what they need to learn in their relationship with God. Because you love them, you will enforce discipline even though it may be painful for you. We have probably all heard a father or mother say to a child, "This is going to hurt me more than it's going to hurt you" prior to an act of discipline. As a kid I always thought, "Give me a break. I know it's going to hurt me more." As parents, unless there's something very twisted in our minds, there is no joy in disciplining a child. Many times you're disciplining yourself as well. But you have to enforce what's right.

The proverb tells us to discipline "promptly." However, this does not mean that it should be done in anger. If you're angry with your child and he is quivering in the corner, that is not the time to discipline. A parent must get control of his temper and feelings first, or he runs the risk of teaching his child something else—lack of self-control! So have a word of prayer. Calm down so you can think clearly. Then go in and talk to him. Here's an exaggerated example: "Hi, son. Now I know you blew up the Porsche by accident. And I want you to know I'm having a hard time understanding it. I didn't know when I got you that chemistry set you'd figure out the whole thing. Now I'm going to have to discipline you." Orderly, controlled, and calm—but effective. This kind of communication is an important part of discipline; it gives your child answers to his questions and builds his respect for you as a parent and a friend.

It's sad, but I must address those who might take these concepts of discipline and use them as a premise for child abuse. Child abuse is now the second leading cause of death among children from birth to age 12. In the last ten years child-abuse cases have gone up 261 percent in Los Angeles County. More than 120,000 California children are reported as abused every year, and 84 percent of juvenile delinquents were victims of abuse.

God does not grant permission to abuse. That has never been the purpose of discipline. In fact, the Ephesians passage tells us not to provoke them to anger lest they become discouraged or have their spirit broken. That's what happens in a lot of homes. The spirit of the child is broken. The father and/or mother go too far, thinking they are raising a child in the way of the Lord when in reality they are turning him away from the Lord. They have not honored biblical teaching on the right way to minister to their children.

There's a man in the Bible named Eli. He was a high priest and a judge of Israel. He neglected his two sons and they went on to live lives of rebellion and disobedience. They knew no absolutes. Ultimately they died, and Eli died as a result of their rebellion against God. Eli's own failure to set guidelines came back to haunt him. God help us to raise our children in the way they should go!

Another challenge in parenting is teaching responsibility. Solomon spoke of this frustration in Ecclesiastes. He was concerned that the labor he had done would be passed on to someone who had no appreciation for what he had accomplished. It's tempting to give your child everything on a silver platter. For instance, it's much easier to clean a child's room than to tell a child to clean his own room. You know he will take an hour to do it when you could do it in 12 minutes. The important thing is that he needs to learn to do it. He needs to learn that it is his responsibility. That's all a part of training, raising, disciplining, instructing, admonishing, and setting a child in the way he should go.

Perhaps you are a parent whose child is now a teenager and is going through a time of rebellion. You may be very frustrated. You may be thinking, "I've tried all of that. To the best of my ability, though I was not a perfect parent, I really put these principles into action." Take heart. The Scripture in Proverbs that I quoted earlier, "Train up a child in the way he should go, and when he is old he will not depart from it," is not a guarantee that your child will not go astray. Let's keep in mind that the perfect parent, God the Father, lost His first two children to sin. He certainly did nothing wrong when He created Adam and Eve and set them in the Garden. They rebelled against Him. They had the choice to do what was right or what was wrong. We can also look at the story of the prodigal son. It would appear that he had everything in a home that someone could want. It would appear that he was loved and cared for. Yet he chose to rebel. It's not always the fault of the parent. There is that foolishness in the heart of a child. Sometimes he has to go out and learn the hard way. Keep praying for him. Keep on unconditionally loving him and letting him know that you love him even when he sins.

I've heard it said, "Do your best; commit the rest." We can only do what we can do, and leave the rest in the hands of God. All of us as parents know how hard it is to raise children in this time. We know all the things that are pulling on them. It's so important to lay a godly foundation in the home. Don't let up. Hold your course. Put these principles into action.

John wrote in his third epistle, "I have no greater joy than to hear that my children walk in truth." He was talking about spiritual children, but it certainly applies to our natural children as well. I can't think of anything that gives me more joy than to see my child grasp the things of God for himself, without me telling him to put them into action. I once saw another boy try to pick a fight with my son. The boy kept taunting, but Christopher wouldn't respond. Finally Christopher told him, "I don't want to fight you. I'm a Christian. I don't need to fight you." Then the kid threw a blow. Christopher stepped back and the kid fell over and rolled down a little hill. He wasn't hurt, but he got nailed. Yet most of all I was glad to see that he knew fighting was senseless. It warms my heart to see our children getting these biblical principles rooted in their own lives.

I find it interesting that Scripture specifically singles out the fathers for this type of discipline and nurture. If you're a father, you're the key in the home. God has placed the responsibility for the family's welfare on your shoulders. One of the biggest complaints I hear is that fathers come home from work with the idea that they have worked hard all day, and that the only thing left for them that evening is dinner and a newspaper. All the while the children suffer. Fathers, take the initiative! Be spiritual leaders to your children. Be godly examples in the home. Be the man that God has called you to be, and carry out these principles.

It's been said, "The best defense is a good offense." In defending our youth against some of the horrible temptations and elements around them, I suggest that you take the offense and spiritually equip them!

By applying biblical principles to our homes we can lay a strong foundation in the lives of our children on which they can build for years to come. We as parents face an uphill battle in today's society as we seek to rear our children with godly values and desires. But God never asks us to do anything He will not give us the strength to do! So let's continue first as parents to live in fellowship with God through Jesus Christ, and then let us consult His "manual for living," the Bible, and yield to His Holy Spirit. In doing so we will be the kind of people who by example and training will equip our children to know our God and to pass on His love and Word to another generation. Consider King David's final words to his son Solomon as he was ready to die: "As for you, my son Solomon, know the God of your father, and serve Him with a loyal heart and with a willing mind; for the Lord searches all hearts and understands all the intent of the thoughts. If you seek Him, He will be found by you" (1 Chronicles 28:9).

I can't think of better advice for parents today than to pass this kind of spiritual legacy to their children. May God help all of us to *know* God and to pass on that knowledge to our children.

Notes

Chapter 2—When Will the Pain Stop?
1. In *Christianity Today*, Mar. 1987, p. 19.
2. Ibid., p. 21.
3. Ibid.
4. *Seventeen*, Apr. 1985.

Chapter 3—Sex, Drugs, and Heavy Metal
1. Jay Kesler, *Parents and Teenagers* (Victor, 1984), p. 507.
2. Ibid.
3. Claudia Wallis, "Children Having Children," in *Time*, Dec. 9, 1985, p. 79.

Chapter 4—Private Battles
1. *Newsweek*, Feb. 11, 1980, p. 58.
2. *Christianity Today*, Mar. 1987.
3. *Newsweek*, Feb. 11, 1980, p. 58.
4. Ibid., p. 59.
5. *USA Today*, Oct. 30, 1986.

Chapter 6—All We Like Sheep
1. James Dobson, *Preparing for Adolescence* (Santa Ana: Vision House, 1978), pp. 46-49.

Chapter 8—Handling Temptation
1. Guttmacher Institute Report, Mar. 1985.
2. "Teen Pregnancy and School-Based Health Clinics" (Family Research Council), p. 1.
3. Kesler, *Parents*, p. 507.
4. *USA Today*, Feb. 6, 1987.

Chapter 9—God's Call to the Young
1. *USA Today*, Oct. 31, 1986.
2. *Los Angeles Times*, Nov. 21, 1986.

Chapter 10—Family in Crisis

1. *U.S. News & World Report*, Dec. 9, 1985.
2. Ibid.
3. Paul Leeton, *Encyclopedia of 7700 Illustrations* (Assurance Publishers, 1979).
4. *Seventeen*, Apr. 1985.
5. "Crime in America" (ABC Report, 1983).
6. *Pulpit Helps*, 1985.
7. *USA Today*, Oct. 1986.

Chapter 11—Help for Parents

1. *Riverside Press*, Nov. 6, 1986.
2. *Focus on the Family*, Mar. 1987.
3. *Pulpit Helps*, June 1985.

Other Good
Harvest House Reading

COMMUNICATION: KEY TO YOUR PARENTS
by *Rex Johnson*
This guide teaches teenagers to build or rebuild the patterns of communication with their families.

COMMUNICATION: KEY TO YOUR TEENS
by *Norm Wright and Rex Johnson*
Practical suggestions for parents for improving and maintaining communication with teenagers.

GOD'S DESIGN FOR CHRISTIAN DATING
by *Greg Laurie*
In the midst of conflicting worldly standards, it is still possible to find and fulfill God's design for exciting relationships with the opposite sex. Offering godly counsel with touches of humor, Greg gives the "how-to" of healthy dating.

PARENTS IN CONTROL
Bringing Out the Best in Your Children
by *David Rice*
Getting your children under control is not as difficult as it might seem. *Parents in Control* explores: 1) How parents get out of control, and 2) How to bring out the best in your child. Written for every parent, whether single or married, *Parents in Control* combines insight with a "nuts and bolts" approach to solving family problems.

PRIVATE PAIN
Healing for Hidden Hurts
by *Rich Wilkerson*
Rich Wilkerson, author of *Teenagers: Parental Guidance Suggested*, tells us that "Few are exempt from some degree of private pain." Private pain may be emotional isolation, a sense of rejection, guilt, loneliness, depression, or other forms of inner anguish kept hidden from people. A powerful book that offers help and understanding and shows how suffering and pain need not devastate us but can be tools in the great Master Sculptor's plan for our lives.

TEENAGERS: PARENTAL GUIDANCE SUGGESTED
by *Rich Wilkerson*

With dynamic impact, well-known youth speaker Rich Wilkerson has captured for parents the secrets of achieving fulfilling relationships with teens. Honest answers for the tough issues we face with our children. Formerly *Hold Me While You Let Me Go*.

Harvest Videos Presents

THE FINAL CRY
with Greg Laurie

This 30-minute, high-quality VHS video takes a powerful and moving look at the complex issues that are contributing to the alarming increase in the number of teenage suicides in the world today. Noted pastor and teacher Greg Laurie, senior pastor of the 6,000-member Harvest Christian Fellowship in Riverside, California, whose teaching is heard throughout the U.S. on his radio program, "A New Beginning," addresses the many profound questions faced by teens and parents alike and discusses vital lessons we all must learn. In graphic but sensitive interviews, Greg takes the viewer into the personal lives of teens who were saved from becoming a part of the shocking death statistic of one teen suicide per hour. Greg offers Christ as the solution!

FOR USE AT HOME...
YOUTH RETREATS...CHURCH...
YOUTH GROUPS...SUNDAY SCHOOL

Available for purchase
or rental at your local Christian bookstore.

About the Author

Greg Laurie is the pastor of Harvest Christian Fellowship, a growing church in Southern California where thousands of people attend each week.

For more than ten years, Greg has been counseling men and women of all ages. He has written several books and speaks extensively on the subject of personal relationships. He is also heard coast-to-coast on his daily radio broadcast.

He is dedicated to bringing the Word of God in a fresh, contemporary style to a generation facing the pressures and challenges of our changing world.

Greg wants to share with you *THE FINAL CRY* and his preventive answers to the tragedy of teen suicide, a topic of vital importance to more than 19 million singles in our country.